To Do List

A Practical Guide To Setting And Achieving Goals

(A Diagrammatic Guide To Complete Your Tasks Within A Weeks)

Corey Riley

Published By **Chris David**

Corey Riley

All Rights Reserved

To Do List: A Practical Guide To Setting And Achieving Goals (A Diagrammatic Guide To Complete Your Tasks Within A Weeks)

ISBN 978-1-77485-552-2

No part of this guidebook shall be reproduced in any form without permission in writing from the publisher except in the case of brief quotations embodied in critical articles or reviews.

Legal & Disclaimer

The information contained in this ebook is not designed to replace or take the place of any form of medicine or professional medical advice. The information in this ebook has been provided for educational & entertainment purposes only.

The information contained in this book has been compiled from sources deemed reliable, and it is accurate to the best of the Author's knowledge; however, the Author cannot guarantee its accuracy and validity and cannot be held liable for any errors or omissions. Changes are periodically made to this book. You must consult your doctor or get professional medical advice before using any of the suggested remedies, techniques, or information in this book.

Upon using the information contained in this book, you agree to hold harmless the Author from and against any damages, costs, and expenses, including any legal fees potentially resulting from the application of any of the information provided by this guide. This disclaimer applies to any damages or injury caused by the use and application, whether directly or indirectly, of any advice or information presented, whether for breach of contract, tort, negligence, personal injury, criminal intent, or under any other cause of action.

You agree to accept all risks of using the information presented inside this book. You need to consult a professional medical practitioner in order to ensure you are both able and healthy enough to participate in this program.

Table of contents

Introduction 1

Chapter 1: The Characteristics Of To-Do Lists... 6

Chapter 2: Power Of The List Power Of The List 12

Chapter 3: The Way To Make To-Do Lists 17

Chapter 4: Popular To-Do List Systems .. 28

Chapter 5: First Things First 32

Chapter 6: Planning Is Important: Make Lists And Utilize The Tools At Your Disposition 37

Chapter 7: What To Do When To Do Routine Work.. 47

(Like Email) 47

Chapter 8: Utilizing The To-Do-List To Create Deadlines And Goals.................... 54

Chapter 9: Define Goals And Motivation 59

Chapter 10: Time Management 66

Chapter 11: Correlation Between Time Management Skills And Success 91

Chapter 12: To Do-List Apps 106

Chapter 13: Timeboxing Vs. Time 123

Chapter 14: How To Do When You First Start 130

Chapter 15: Importance Of Taking Breaks 143

Chapter 16: Time Management The Relationship Between Productivity And Success - What's The Link? 148

Chapter 17: The Habits Of Effective Time Managers 177

Conclusion 183

Introduction

Imagine someone calling you for assistance with being overwhelmed. Someone might respond, "I always have much to accomplish however I'm not sure what to do and then I ignore it." What do you think of your response to the conversation? Do you think it would sound like:" you know what? I was feeling the same way, however I've not felt that way since a few years and I'm going to tell you the things that have changed and the changes that are taking place in my personal life, so that I'm not suffering from that issue no more."

You could also be the one who requires an aid in resolving this issue. The best part is that I'll give you tried and tested techniques for deciding on a task before time by making an effective list of things to do.

The most important thing to keep in mind is the reason you create to-do lists at all in the first place, which is to take the tasks off your mind and the issues that they bring and free up your valuable brain to focus on more important tasks.

This is a blend of methods that I've combined to create a checklist that is effective:

Use Paper for Short-Term Goals

Digital tools, according to me can be used to plan for long durations that are time-bound, and to plan bigger projects. But they come with a major drawback which makes them a bad choice for planning your day-to-day activities because they're never-ending. They don't give you any idea of the state of your planning while a paper-based list can be used as an indicator of your day.

You should be able to use no more than a single piece of paper that has a couple of lines to make your agenda. This will make you prioritize. Things that aren't important will not be able to make it the list since you don't have the time to do everything.

Additionally, paper permits the marking off items in a more pleasing way than a digital one which means you are able to proceed into the next category.

Have a go at cherry-picking

It could sound like an untruthful advice but I promise you, it's awe-inspiring.

You have something important on your to-do list that you'd like to accomplish. It might be simple and quick. Do that task first. The sooner you are able to cross off something particularly the most important items more efficiently. The brain releases dopamine whenever you do something. This is a neurohormone which can, help you become more efficient. This method is known as priming.

There's no need to complete the list.

It appears to be against something I said earlier and that is the fact that your checklist is your goal-setting bar for the day. So how do one not be a complete fail if you get only two items completed on your list within one day? The way I approach it is. You take a look at the incomplete list and don't let it stop you.

You can only accomplish all you can accomplish in a day, regardless of how long your list.

Effectively and efficiently completing your list for the next time

If you have to create an entirely new list, make sure you shift those items that are essential and remove those that aren't. It is a good idea to determine which items are in the category of not important, and you should avoid these things. We now have a clean and fresh list of essential items on it.

Let's get to what might become the single most crucial point of all.

Create little shadow boxes.

When you're creating a checklist, make a small box beside each major item, and then fill in a small empty checkbox. Then, as you've finished your list, return to each box, and draw a drop shadow.

Making a small drop shadow is a tranquil kind of mini-meditation practice. It's calming and calm, and comes with three benefits:

In the beginning, there is the the dopamine rush associated with marking items off because you must mark boxes as well.

Then, as you get into a state of meditation this will allow your mind the opportunity to concentrate on and process the things on your list.

Like clockwork, when you're in this states, new and crucial items will appear in your mind.

Chapter 1: The Characteristics of To-Do Lists.

Many of us have different methods of to-do lists. However, organizational experts have found that certain ways to put a productive list out are superior to others.

However, there are some the common traits of the best to-do lists that help us to be productive and ease the stress we feel.

Here are 10 characteristics of the top to-do lists based on studies of hundreds of lists throughout time, and also from the most current research and literature on the topic.

Very serious work of preparation

The most effective lists of things to do begin with taking a few minutes to record everything you must complete. If you'd like to do this method, choose a particular date to plan your schedule. Most business professionals prefer to plan for each quarter of the year, while Others live their lives according to the seasons. Some prefer to plan a month in advance or a week ahead, while others prefer a month. It is estimated that in order to complete this task as experts do It will take between 1 and 2 hours.

Task break down

When all the tasks are set out, you can study the tasks to determine what's required. Are they one-act-only tasks or multifaceted, complex tasks? If they belong to the latter category, they must be broken into as small steps as is feasible.

Specific information

For instance the agenda of the extremely efficient list writer doesn't contain the words "Meet to Jack on 9 a.m. It simply says "meet with Jack Bring the coffee and cream but and no sugar, and convince the writer to accept the content on his website. Make sure you negotiate at least three more weeks in terms of timing before a model of the website needs to be displayed."

Prioritization

We often consider prioritization as numbers 1, 2, 3, and so on. although that's great for lists that are used daily however, for longer-term lists it can be more beneficial to indicate whether it is essential, important but not urgent, or if it is needed, but not urgent nor vital. You can use your own code or using the initials U I and NU could be sufficient.

The ability to adapt to your lifestyle

It is a highly controversial topic in the field of the making of lists. The scientific evidence suggests that shorter daily lists of not more than three or four items work best for most people. However, when it comes to your own personal life don't let yourself be governed by rules set by others. Determine what works best for you. Many managers who need to manage multiple projects realize that having a larger list of tasks that guarantee some improvement is made each day. It is less stressful than having to choose only three projects per day to tackle.

Plan ahead

The most frequent characteristic of successful to-do listers is their determination that they never end a day without planning for the next. You might decide that marking off your priority items for the coming day will end your day with ease at work and you might find that your ability to take decisions and concentrate more clearly is after you've reached the calm at the end of your day. Whatever system is most effective for you is acceptable. In any case, you'll get your day started better if you make sure that your list of priorities is done and ready to be completed upon waking.

Technology or paper of your choice

It's all an individual decision. Many who utilize the classic list writing skill of putting pen to paper experience an euphoria and control while they perform their daily lists. Others find it to be easier to utilize the simplest Microsoft Word document list or one of the other electronic options ranging from "Evernote" up to "Toodledo" and even "Remember the milk".

Unique solutions

The president or the prime minister For instance, they have an extensive list of tasks to be able to move forward than average people. They may require more sophisticated software that can handle some of their scheduling , and regularly send out alerts. If your life is becoming too complicated, you should consider an organizational solution that is specifically tailored to your needs.

Life's transitions can be a challenge.

Our typical days are comprised of things is done for us as well as for others. We effortlessly master the process of completing our personal grooming needs and preparing breakfast for our own and for others taking care of a colleague and heading to work working on our tasks and remembering to contact at the end of the day to inquire about a sick family member or a coworker for lunch, then hurrying to home an hour early to make it to the technician to fix our air conditioner.

What makes the to-do lists of highly effective individuals is their understanding that life must flow smoothly through different segments in order in order to make a seamless. Instead of just focusing on the work-related tasks, they note their other important events, understanding that in order for our lives to run efficiently, we need to be able to connect every aspect of it.

Techniques that are individualized

List-making is, as those who practice it will be able to prove it, is the process of recollecting the tasks that must be accomplished, deciding on what is most important and then completing the task that are in front of you. Many report that one of one of the most challenging aspect of the three main pillars in list-making involves making a decision on what is most crucial.

Certain people have developed unique strategies to help them determine which items should be first in their lists. They ask themselves: What of my tasks should I not complete it today will bring me most stress in the future? Some ask: Which task will bring the most money associated with it, or has the highest satisfaction from personal achievement. Develop your own system of assessment in accordance with your own personal beliefs and that it is much simpler to make the choice.

Chapter 2: Power Of The List Power Of The List

With a myriad of options all over the world that range from extravagant iPhone applications to calendars and beyond, I've never come across something that is as powerful, flexible and useful as a simple to-do list.

There are four main motives to make a list of things to do:

In the first place, it is an affirmation of my best and most efficient usage of time.

Yes, it's a list with things I must finish... However, it's much more than the scope of. When I write down my daily goals in a specific way I am always evaluating every opportunity I am presented with throughout the day with an extremely powerful lens: that of my desires. Based on my experiences working with hundreds of thousands of clients one-on one, as well as in workshops and in groups We spend little time thinking about our goals.

We think about the future. We think about what we'll fund college tuition, the items items we'll should buy at the store to prepare dinners in the next week or if it's time to change the oil filter. However, we do not think about the brightest possible future. We're so focused on the present and what's about to take place tomorrow and next week that the bigger things are put off. The problem with this is that we can't seem to be able to tackle it. A list of things to do, created and utilized in the manner I'll show you, will help bring those golden, shining dreams out of the box inside the closet and out into the open and onto the scene of today. You'll be excited when you realize how simple it is to build the future you've always fantasized about.

Second, people get distracted. There are millions and millions of demands to be attended to every day. Being reminded of what you're focusing on throughout the day will bring you back and again. There's no reason to delay writing the next chapter of your book simply because it was something you "forgot." The idea was before your eyes, something that you considered many times throughout the duration of the day.

A third, a list of things to do is a simple black and white (sometimes literally) review of the extent to which you're doing the things you should be doing. If your to-do list has been made in a way that is correct, at time of completion, it acts as a measurement of the last 24 hours. It is commonplace to are able to go about our lives without feedback. Are we doing a great job as a mother? A good employee? A successful business owner? A good human? It's not easy to discern.

However, when you have your list of things to refer to and those check marks or strikethroughs in the list of things you've accomplished, you'll be able to give yourself a pat on the back and lay your head down on your pillow knowing you've accomplished what you're supposed to
accomplish. (Secret not to tell that I occasionally check back through old lists of things to do for a reason to keep myself motivated and to assure myself that I'mn't simply consuming oxygen in this world. I'm actually getting major things completed - and I've got evidence!)

The fourth one could be the most crucial for you. To-do lists simply can be effective. When you adhere to my method to create and use your own personal to-do lists it will help you accomplish more than you could have imagined. You'll be more focused, productive and effective. The most efficient group since Crosby, Stills and Nash made their last album.

Chapter 3: The Way To Make To-Do Lists

That Produces Results

The purpose of a to-do list is to get tasks accomplished. Strangely enough, most people spend more time planning their tasks instead of getting things done.

It's essential to adhere to this advice as it's very easy to spend a lot of time planning your day, and too little time actually doing things. This is why we'll discuss this in the next section. we'll put everything in an action plan which focuses on helping you achieve results.

Step 1: Select the To-Do List platform

There are two options in managing your list of tasks:

*1. Paper approach with hard copies stored in an envelope.

*2. Digital checklists of things to do that sync between your computer or mobile (like apps like the Remember the Milk app.)

The decision is really all up to you. I like the paper method since I enjoy having a binder with all of my work and projects in the future, no matter where I am working. However you may like the ability to sync, and multi-platform capabilities of a digital task list. No matter what you choose it is important to engage with this software and make use of it regularly.

Step 2: Make use of Evernote to record ideas

Evernote is among the few productivity apps I regularly use on a basis. It's likely that you're overwhelmed with ideas. It's important to establish an environment where you can keep track of your ideas regularly. With Evernote you can keep track of thoughts and notes throughout the day, and take notes of important articles when working on a computer. The entire collection can be saved in one central location for simple access.

3. Make Personal Lists of Personal and Professional Project Lists

Anything that requires several steps should be incorporated in a list of projects. This can be saved in a physical folder , or in your electronic to-do lists.

4. Do an Weekly Review

Schedule an hour each week to think about the coming seven
days. Sundays are my favorite because I'm relaxed after a long weekend and more energized to take on the coming week.

Concentrate on completing one or two tasks during this time:

- Determine your routine and appointments. It is better to be aware beforehand whether your week is full of meetings and appointments. This way, you don't have to squeeze in numerous activities. If you do, it will only make you feel dissatisfied and unproductive. Prior obligations should be added to your weekly list of things to do prior to the project's tasks.

- Schedule project tasks. Select the most important projects for the next 7 days. Plan out the time that you will be able to work on certain tasks. Add them to your daily to-do list, and treat them as prioritised schedules.

Identify the energy levels you require. Note down a number, ranging from one (low) up to five (high)--next to each item on the weekly agenda. This number should correspond to the level of energy required to finish the task. Set the tasks in a way that they correspond to your own circadian rhythms.

Process ideas you have gathered. Check all records (from Evernote or the 43 Folders system). Write a quick list of projects of what you'll be doing for each idea, and then schedule an appointment to follow-up on the idea. This is crucial because you'll not miss out on an opportunity.

That's it!

After you've completed your daily review, you'll be able to create a plan that acts as a rough plan of action for the following seven days. Make sure you include flexibility as you never know when an emergency might make you change your routine.

Action 5: Begin Every Day by reading MITs

With your daily to-do list as a starting point, list the three things that will most impact your life. Note the tasks down on an Post-It notepad or a tiny index cards. Begin each day by doing these tasks prior to doing any other task. These must be clearly defined with specific stopping and starting dates. Additionally, you should select one that will measure the accomplishment of each step.

Additionally, you should plan for breaks during your work. Take this time to unwind and stretch, stroll around, or grab an espresso. This is essential as it helps you recharge your batteries prior to focusing on your next task.

Action 6 Step 6: Simply Do It!

This is the one that's often most difficult for people. Everyone experiences the initial feeling of inertia just before beginning the working day. What can you do? Just focus on the first step to get to work. Here are some ideas that may help:

- Remove distractions. This includes ringing and dinging technologies like email instant messaging, social media texts and calls to the phone. Distractions may also take form in the form of clutter on your desktop as well as background noise and multitasking. You should begin the day by focusing on your most important work.

Make plans. It's easy for us to put off projects if we'ren't ready to complete the task. When you're not equipped with all the documents emails, documents or programs then you'll be spending time searching for the items. The trick to solving this issue is to organize everything prior to time (like the day prior) so that you are able to start working.

Start by committing to starting. Don't think about how much effort is required to finish the task. Instead, focus on meeting an extremely small goal or significant milestone. This is based on the mentality of the mini habit concept that I have mentioned earlier. Once you start the task, momentum often begins to build and you'll keep moving forward.

Concentrate on "The Present." Don't get caught up in the numerous tasks that have to be accomplished at the time the day is over. Do not worry about failing or what could occur. Just focus on doing the very best job you can within the time allocated to the job.

Plan for the obstacles. It's a good idea to record what's going through your head every time you're stuck. Are you unsure of the task to accomplish? Do you have a doubt about the best way to complete something? Do you fear of failing? The most effective way to conquer any obstacle is to pinpoint the reason behind your situation and develop a plan to overcome it.

Be aware of the benefits. When everything other options fail, remind yourself that the value in the long run is the task you've completed to you. The more you are able to tie actions to a significant objective, the more inspired you'll be to continue taking actions.

Many struggle to develop"the "getting established routine." The best advice I can offer is to Begin each day by eliminating all distractions, and make a point of completing a list of tasks that are essential to build an upward energy throughout your day.

Action 7 Step 7: Complete daily activities and appointments

Based on the time of day, you'll be required to perform daily activities. My suggestion is to make an agenda of your priorities. Each day, start with your most important MITs Then, you can work on tasks that are just as important. Continue this process until you're done with tasks that need to be completed, but won't mean the most important if not done.

For instance Social media is a crucial aspect for my company, however I do not consider it an "end-of-the-day routine" since it's not as crucial as writing, composing content, or answering emails sent by clients.

Step 8: Take hard Choices

If an item is on your agenda for more than three calendar days it's essential to complete three things:

*1. Begin the next day by making the change immediately before you start anything else.

*2. Set a date on your calendar for you to act on it.

*3. Remove it if it's no any longer needed.

One of the issues that people face when it comes to their lists of tasks is that they are constantly adding tasks and don't eliminate old ideas. In the end, people feel guilty that they've never completed tasks that are years old.

There is an easy (but complicated) solution to this issue Make a hard decision about every task that you have on your agenda. If you put things off, you must immediately act on it or eliminate it. This shouldn't be an overwhelming task. Determine the reason why you've put off certain tasks in your to-do list rather than simply ignoring them.

Action 9: Practice Continuous Improvement

There is no way to make a to-do-list process flawless from the beginning. Truthfully, I'm still working on the way I manage my personal productivity. There are times when you may realize that certain information contained that is in this book may not be relevant to your own life. My suggestion? Choose what you find personally beneficial and leave the rest.

When you're done with your day, the to-do list you are employing should be a reflection of the routine you follow on a regular basis. It is important to try various strategies for managing time and learn from your experience every day and constantly tweaking the method.

Chapter 4: Popular To-Do List Systems

Task + starting date + closing due date

Even if circumstances outside of your control haven't given you a deadline however, you must set an internal time frame for each task you are working on in order to help you make the task more manageable in your head and to improve the likelihood that the project is completed in time.

Master list and daily list

There are tasks we all do that require constant effort. These aren't an all-in-one project. They're tasks which must be accomplished regularly. Examples include processing emails calling, processing phone calls, and doing around. Additionally, you must deal with appointments, meetings as well as personal commitments. These things should be included in a document referred to as"a "weekly to-do list."

Routine chores make up the majority of your time So it's essential to make plans for them and include them in your calendar. It's also important not to get caught in the trap of making a list of every second in your schedule. This will transform your daily schedule into a lengthy and exhausting routine which can cause unnecessary stress.

My suggestion is to record three categories of items to include on your weekly schedule routine tasks that require reinforcement like new habits, appointments, meetings, and personal obligations; crucial tasks that you have taken from your task lists.

1 - 3 - 5 rules

The 1-3-5 rule allows you to complete nine tasks within a single day. This approach lets you complete all the tasks that you must complete and break them down into smaller tasks. It is possible to start with a larger project, then move on to the following three medium-sized projects and then finish with the five small leftovers. If you can complete all of your 1-3-5 tasks within a day, you can end the day by preparing your 1-3-5 tasks for the next day.

Kanban method

Every project is an accumulation of a vast variety of smaller processes that add to larger ones, which can then be added to an even larger one, and then on. Certain of these processes are simple and simple, while others require time and effort. Implementing these processes in a clear sequence is the main goal of every project, as we are aware of.

Kanban is a method of controlling, defining, and improving the execution of these procedures that allows for an efficient work release. Kanban is a catalyst in companies and encourages rapid and more targeted change within. The ease at the process of change can reduce resistance, and provides more value to the overall organization and facilitates efficient execution. In the end, the capacity to adjust to changes is crucial to the organization's success.

The Kanban approach focuses on creating an understanding of what might otherwise be viewed as not-knowledge work. The purpose behind this is to make sure that the whole process is in the right level of responsibility. It is important to note that there shouldn't be any work that is requested by the client which isn't fulfilled. In essence it is the Kanban method is an flow-based delivery system that helps reduce the amount of work that is in the process (WIP) by making usage of visible signals.

Other ways to make a list of things to do include:

Massive, all-inclusive list

3+2 strategy

System based on project

Matrix system

Doing things

Chapter 5: First Things First

If you've learned the power of a checklist, you're likely to start the process of revamping your own checklist. However, let's push the camera back before we get into the day-to-day. To allow our list of things to be moving us in the right direction we must know what the best direction is!

Check out where you are at the moment. If you're in the bedroom (like you are) or in the office or the local Starbucks You're likely to be receiving a myriad of calls that need your attention today. While I look around my bedroom, I notice laundry that has to be cleaned (always!) and my nephew's laptop and school textbooks that have to be put away, a pile of books to read and dogs to take walks and lift hand weights and Facebook. Facebook is always there!

How do we come to discern what the best items are at any moment in the future? It is important to begin at the top, and begin with our top priority -

our goals or our "grand visions" as I refer to them. It is essential to begin by defining precisely what you would like your future to look like in Technicolor and complete with Dolby surround audio and 3D.

Nowadays, people pick a word to represent the year or even create an intention such as "beauty," "grace," or "fly." If you've fallen in line with this fashion It's a great feeling to choose a word represents your year. Perhaps you purchase an engraved necklace, and you may even decorate your walls and then you are excited to tell your friends about what you're planning for the next 12 months and that's usually where the story ends.

In the end, how are you able to bring "fly" as well as "breathe" out from the air into the every day? What can you do to make it something you can actually do? It's a challenge and that's why we tend to lose track of our words (or your resolutions) at some point in springtime.

Don't be afraid. I've got an alternative to the fleeting. I'll assist you to set goals and create goals that can be achieved But first, let's discuss prioritization. You've probably figured out that I'm a word-nerd and I prefer to begin by defining words.

I am awestruck by the fact how priority is something that is considered to be being more significant, and not only things we say have more importance. 2

When we talk regarding priorities, the topics that pop up the most frequently are the ones I call "The Five Fs:"

*Faith

*Family

*Friends

*Fitness

*Finances

Other values that are common to all include creativity, community and leadership, as well as relationships authenticity, and much more.

They're all wonderful terms... But how do you go about taking, like, "relationships," and add it to your to-do list? There's nothing you can do that's not possible, and as we've talked about this, an agenda is something you can accomplish. That's the biggest gap between the dream and intention and the day-to-day.

We usually have an idea of what we want in a vague, enjoyable long-term way however, we aren't sure how to achieve it. We are aware of what our priorities are or what "one word" is but we're not sure that we're clear about what we're looking for. When we get to the point at which we can claim that our primary goal will be "relationships," we're still uncertain of where we're heading since, although we're aware the concept of "relationships" are crucial to us There are millions of different kinds of relationships. There are even millions of kinds of good relationships!

In the end, it can be difficult and frustrating to make progress towards the goal of the future. In the spring, we have March or April and we put our goals and plans aside and return cleaning laundry or addressing questions on the top of the email inbox. There's enough of it to keep us engaged.

If you're fed up of this and trying your best but not seeing the results you've always wanted to make and want to, then let's continue. Now is the time to take the first step towards achieving your agenda by deciding your top priorities.

Task: Take five minutes to record your most important three to five top priorities. Don't be concerned over the priority order (if "health" is prior to or follows "faith," for instance). Don't fret about having a hard time settling them all it's only a beginning point.

Do not fret whether your priorities differ from what they were one or two years or two ago. In different times in our lives, things could be moved up or down our priorities list. There is no static. your lifestyle changes, and your priorities shift. That's GOOD. Take a moment to think about the present as well as now, and what you're most concerned about now. It's just a snapshot in time Don't let it cause you to stress. I'm teaching you a method that you can refer back to time and time again.

Keep in mind that there aren't "right" and "wrong" priority and they are entirely yours and do not require justification or defense.

Chapter 6: planning is Important: Make Lists and Utilize the Tools at Your Disposition

One wise person once stated that the plan is not important while the planning process is essential. We all have plans for some thing. It's a fantastic method to get a better understanding of the goals you have set for yourself. However, what we don't know is that you must establish the course of your plans, otherwise it could become a beautiful image to be viewed but be that is buried at the rear of your head.

Making lists is the most effective method of staying on the right path. The route to a specific target may appear clear at first but then you realize you've found yourself at the center of the plan, crammed with work, paperwork and those who ask you questions that take more time and effort from you. These obstacles can cause you headaches and divert you from your goals.

Start creating lists. Not just lists of tasks - every kind of list. The diary is a kind of habit of keeping lists as is the list of grocery items on your fridge. You're aware of how useful your journal is in trying to remember what you last fought with your pal was Let's look at various kinds of lists to help you decide the one that will save your life:

Shopping Lists - they are necessary for every household. You'll want to write down everything you'll need to buy when you get the last thing from the fridge. Make a chalkboard in your kitchen to place stickers on or place them in a stack in the refrigerator itself. As time passes, you'll know what items you will need to purchase weekly and those that you purchase monthly. It is possible to create tables in your computer which include the items you purchase every week, and then you can add new items under the weekly categories.

Another stress-inducing and time-consuming problem we frequently face is shopping for gifts. The holidays of Christmas, Mother's Day, Father's Day you know what. What's the harm in trying to think of gifts in advance. Keep your notebook to be prepared in the event that you stumble across something you think someone in you know would like. It's possible that you don't remember every gift idea you've come across over the course of the year, but when a major event such as the New Year's holiday or birthday occurs it's easy to pull your notebook and use it as a reference sheet.

Checklists: These kinds of lists can be useful for those who need to be ready for an appointment or an event. Stress can cause you to forget, so you should keep the necessary items you require for an event or event. Let's say you need to make to give a presentation to give. Your checklist should include all the items you'll need to be successful. The items you need to include could be:

*Copies of the outline of the project

The product is modeled after the model.

*Laptop, slides and so on.

*Spare batteries or a power cable

*Pens: blue, red and black

*Lucky charm

Resource Lists - If you discover a source of information to be reliable in terms of statistical accuracy and meets your needs, make sure it is classified. We live in a new century, so make use of the tools that are at our available. You can make multiple folders within your browser that are named differently (e.g. recipes or news, entertainment films, others.) which means you can accelerate your search whenever you're most in need of it.

A lot of browsers allow you to create multiple users. You can choose to name one "Work" for use those who work; and yet another user is named "Home" to be used browsing for pleasure as well as you can create one user for each member of your family who uses the same computer, ensuring that your history of browsing and analytics do not cross.

It can be of huge advantage if you create an account on Google email account only for work. This way, if your boss requires a log of your activities at work or wants to know the origin of the data then you simply login to your account and look up the sources that you utilized. If you're the boss, make sure that everyone in your company to use your email address to monitor their performance.

A list of ideas - We have ideas throughout the day, but typically only you can only remember a few or none in certain instances. There are numerous occasions that you come across something that makes you want to take a different path of actions. Sometimes, it's an idea to examine a aspect from a different angle or perhaps the phrase you wanted to know occurred to you as you washed your hands while using the toilet. Note this information in a notebook , and then look over it daily.

Money Lists This is a challenging one, especially if do not have the organizational skills. Making a list of every expense will be noted, will provide you with solid proof that where the money is going. For this to be successful ensure you have receipts for every purchase. If you have lost your receipt, record the purchase down on your smartphone or a notebook. When you are done with your month when you've calculated your totals, you'll find out how much you've spent on bills, food entertainment, and taxes. As time passes, you'll discover what is essential and what you can leave out. These kinds of lists help attention to the bigger picture and provide you with an idea of what you could reduce your expenses.

Goal lists These are the most complicated lists that require special focus. It is necessary examine each item individually, and then calculate the amount of time and resources you'll need to reach these goals. Setting a goal, and creating an action plan to achieve it will inspire you and unleash all your potential. If you don't, you could be wasting your energy and time to achieve your own dreams and accomplishments.

Based on the Zeigarnik Effect, humans tend to recall things they haven't done over the work they've already done. This is why it's ideal to have the notebook you use on your smartphone or in your purse to record both the things you've done before and the information you think that you'll forget in the future. The first one will allow you maintain a record of all your completed objectives. According to the Zeigarnik effect that we tend to forget about the things we have completed and this will serve as an excellent reminder of what you've done during the week or day. Sometimes, when the days are so hectic that you're not sure whether you've got your head in your hands, and yet it feels like you haven't done any thing. Make a list of the tasks you have completed and you'll be amazed at how much you're actually able to accomplish.

A variety of tools are accessible when you put in the effort to prepare for the future. From the traditional notebook and pen recording, to the latest mobile applications that can simplify your life simpler. There's even a specially made device designed for creating lists and keeping contact information on the go, which is known as the personal digital assistant, or PDA. It's no longer very well-known due to the fact that mobile phones can be equipped to support more sophisticated applications.

Nowadays, virtual assistants and applications provide a wide range of choices. It is possible to assign different colours to every type of job in the calendar to make them easy to find without having to look through every. For instance, you can assign red for meetings, and green to events, blue for phone calls, and sending email. The program may be able to group various types of tasks according to priority categories, date or category. The majority of applications allow you to remind you prior to completing a task and set the time that your application is going to remind you of it, e.g. three hours prior to the deadline and a day or week, others. The best part is that today's devices can connect to the internet Don't forget to utilize Google Drive, Dropbox and similar platforms to save and share photos, documents, and documents at any time you're required to.

It is advisable to create all kinds of lists and employ different kinds of assistants. Install a virtual assistant on your list of tasks throughout the day, and for tasks associated with your task at hand. Keep a notebook in your purse or pocket to record those little things that you have to think of throughout the day. Install a chalkboard near your refrigerator and record the things you've used up. Utilize the recording function on your smartphone to record items you aren't able to record at the moment. We do not count the few seconds we take to note something down however, when the time arrives, you'll realize that you have saved time. Time that you could use to enjoy your life to the fullest.

Chapter 7: What to do when to Do Routine Work

(Like Email)

Email is an ongoing activity. The issue with taking a break at every 5 minutes or so to check your emails is that your time is time you could be using for more productive tasks. Of course you must respond to your emails promptly however, you shouldn't have to constantly stray from the work you want to do on your list of things to do to accomplish this. If you do, you'll find that they create chaos and aren't very productive because they get distracted. Therefore, you should establish a time when you will check and reply to emails every day.

It is important to know how to use your email the best way possible. If you allocate an amount of time for email, the best thing you can do is create an automated answer system so that people know that you'll be following with them when you're able to. You can alter the message frequently, which is simple to set up and takes a couple of minutes, but should they receive a response from you, then at the very least they'll be pleased. The language I employ in my email is standard and I have an existing Word document that has all the text so I don't need to write it every time:

Thank you for contacting me via email. Please be aware that I am working However, I will be back to you soon.

This is a standard procedure however, you can enhance it or even make it more specific in the event that you set a date and time that you respond to emails:

Thank you for sending me an email. I check my emails every day at around 10:30 a.m. and will reply to your message within the next hour. If, during the meantime it is urgent then you are able to contact me using my mobile phone number.

The goal for these notecards is to certain that your clients are aware that their message has been read. You must then figure out how to incorporate time in your schedule to handle emails with no distractions to be able to quickly get through them and clean out your inbox. Keep in mind that multi-tasking isn't likely to be helpful when you have other things to finish. Therefore, set your time every day to check your emails. This can be the first thing in the morning, when you get to work and after you have returned from lunch.

Go through the email, looking through each one to determine the urgency that the message conveys. There will be some emails which you can respond to quickly and without thinking about it. That can reduce the number of emails you've got down once you've completed the ones you can handle. Take care of those that you have a solution and are able to handle without leaving your desk in order to obtain more details. Finally, take care of those lengthy emails or emails that require some more research before you are able to respond. It is important to ensure that the system you use to file emails is effective and that you've got details at the tip of your fingertips. It's not worth going through a plethora of emails to find the one that contains the details you need. If you separate them into distinct boxes and be able to locate them and you will save a lot of time.

To help you save some time There are a few options you can take. For instance the greeting that appears in the beginning of an email is pretty typical. If you record the kinds of things you type, you'll keep a single file that contains typical email templates. And if you are using an email platform like CRM, it is possible to insert the template whenever you reply to an email. If you don't have CRM, you can create an additional file that contains all this information, but be sure to create your email in a way that your signature from a professional is included in it since it will save you lots of time.

Routine bulk doesn't need to take all that long if you keep yourself organized. If you are unable to answer the problem of someone else, don't waste time in writing back to them by telling them:

I'm not sure. I'll look on it and then get back to you.

The answer you provide is not professional. answer. It is better to recommend a colleague who will be able to answer the question and send a response to the client in the form of:

Your email was passed on to my friend, ………. …………, whom I will respond to you shortly. For your information, his email address is ……………………………….

In doing this, you're getting this off your list of tasks and in reality, it will never be on your list of things to do. You can let your colleague be in charge and your work is completed on this project and you'll have nothing left to do.

It's a far more sensible method of handling email and ensures that you don't wasted your time with things you aren't sure of the answer to. The time wasted searching for answers is a amount of time. When you are ready to respond to your emails, make sure you answer them. Don't talk on IM. Do not put any of them off until later, as the time will not always be the case. Set up your automatic replies in a way that they can continue until you're sitting in your chair, returning to your email.

This provides you with confidence as you know you've handled everything that has come through and that those that write you after the session will receive the opportunity to reply, even if it says to let them be patient. This is better than not acknowledging them in any way and keeps everyone content.

Other routine tasks

It's not the only task you'll need to manage and if you're able to organize your emails into piles of priority it will help. When handling documents, it is best to keep a pile of papers that can be easy to handle, one which needs input from other people and those that require immediate attention. Do the work early in the morning. Then, when you have time spare after you've got your emails finished, get to the pile of paperwork that's simple to handle as you can make the pile smaller and manageable. If there's papers or articles that require additional input from other people you can use the smartphone camera and forward the images to them. It takes only a few seconds. You can also note the area to indicate you did it and follow-up later. This way all you're left with is that one thing that requires your attention and is simple to handle when you're energetic. So, taking having a break or just after your meal is the best timing. At the time you've finished your day, your paperwork as well as your emails must have been taken care of and you should have a your desk clean for your next morning. Likewise, any other items that were not taken care of should be added to your calendar, with an alert to allow you to incorporate it into your agenda for the coming day.

Chapter 8: Utilizing the To-Do-List To Create Deadlines and Goals

Why is it important to set objectives and timelines? What will it do for you? A goal is something you would like to achieve in the near future. It could be a either long-term or short-term goal, and could be as simple as a desire to finish your work in time. If you don't have a vision of something you'd like to accomplish, you will never ever be able to achieve anything. It's not important to you whether you arrive at work 10 minutes later or are 30 minutes late. You'll just continue to drift through your day. However If you have goals you'd like to accomplish and a time frame within which you'd like to achieve your goal, you'll feel an underlying sense of purpose for your day. This feeling of motivation will motivate you to set more goals, as you experience the satisfaction of successfully getting the things done that are on your to-do list.

Making a list of tasks for setting deadlines and goals can be a great method to break down more ambitious goals into actionable items. There are many tasks in your daily life that cannot be accomplished in one day for a normal person, or even being a mother who works. There are certain days you aren't able to write the bills and then update your checkbook in a single day to-do list. You might need to bills in the checkbook the day before. The next day could require you to document receipts into your checkbook. The third day could require updating the balance of your checkbook. It's all based on else you need to complete the day before and your time limits. If you're also planning an activity at school on the evening you plan to pay the bill, don't set yourself up to fail. Many failures can chip away at your self-esteem and lead you to quit on establishing goals. Don't forgo sleep. Lack of sleep can affect you goals and objectives for upcoming day, leading to a cycle of frustration and exhaustion.

There are also things that cannot be accomplished in a single day. You can't put finish your degree on a one day to-do list. If it's the day of your graduation ceremony and all you need to do is sit at home until you receive your diploma. However, even the case, you cannot determine when your diploma will be delivered in the mail. If you'd like to prove that you earned your degree on that day, you'll need attend the ceremony, which will require various actions to be completed before being permitted to walk across the stage and receive your certificate.

The smallest of tasks like cleaning out my basement, compared to your graduation may not be able be accomplished in one day. If I don't get a vacation day, my kids are home by evening, and I'm not a fan of sleeping (ah I really need sleep) and it's almost impossible to finish this huge task without breaking it down into smaller steps. Some may think that this is an exaggeration. My basement isn't even finished! Two storage lockers stuffed inside an 1800 square foot basement stuffed with half-opened boxes, with contents spilling onto the floor.

The primary goal is to establish the objective you'd want to achieve. Once your goal is identified, break it into actionable steps you'll have to accomplish in order to accomplish the desired goal. If you're working towards a long-term kind of goal, those actionable steps must break them down into smaller steps. Once you've got all the items broken down and sorted out, you'll be in a position to determine what you can do every day to accomplish your goal in the near future. Every item that is marked off of your list of things to do can bring your one more step towards achieving your ultimate target.

The idea of breaking your goals down into small, achievable steps can help you to not let the goal go before you give yourself the chance of success.

The most important thing to remember is:

There are certain goals that cannot be accomplished in one sitting. Utilizing your list of to-dos for setting deadlines and goals can be a useful method of breaking larger goals down into action items that can be easily managed.

Once you've determined a objective you'd like to achieve, break that goals into actions you'll be required to follow to achieve your goal.

Every day find one thing you can accomplish that can help you achieve your goal in the near future.

Chapter 9: Define Goals and Motivation

It's difficult to improve your time management and change habits without having personal goals for the changes. If your behavior is a source of irritation to your spouse, your boss or your peers but that's not enough.

What do you want to gain from a better organization? More money, greater recognition in your work or among your family or friends or, simply, a better quality of your life?

All of the above goals and a host of others could be enough to motivate a person to make important improvements to their productivity as well as organizational structure. But, there is a need: goals that are only for you and your own.

Goals with SMART

Once you've found your motivation for trying to master the mastery of lists of tasks, and also with the to-do list of your entire life is now in the process of determining how to work towards

SMART goals. That's right, goals that you should set and also have an important meaning that you can attribute to every target you set.

These are goals:

* Specific The Five W's are the key in this case. It is important that you are able to answer Who is, What, When, Where and why.

Measurable - Determine an appointment ahead of time to know whether you've met your objectives, or a certain "yardstick" should you choose to determine if you've accomplished the things you wanted to accomplish.

* Achievable - With your timetable, and the various aspects of your life, do you imagine yourself achieving this? If you're not, then it's time to revise your draft.

* Relevant - The goals you make are set intended to benefit you. Don't aim to get an award in a field you're not keen on to impress anyone. Make

things that you are happy about and establish goals in line with them.

"Timely." A time-frame to complete the task and the capability to state, "Yes, I definitely succeeded in achieving that goal" are required here.

Another method to define goals, as described in the book Made to Stick by Chip Heath and Dan Heath, is SUCCES which is also known as sticky goals. The goals include:

Simple - The base concept can be easily shared.

* Unexpected - out of the ordinary , or not "the normal."

* Concrete - Concepts with many details tend to stick the most. Stories that have been passed down across generations are excellent examples.

"Credible" - It is possible that you may be sure that it occurred to another person.

* Emotional Stories: You identify with the characters that are in the tale.

Now , you're asking how can this set of guidelines apply to your to-do list objectives? It's as simple as that: these kinds of goals will grab your interest. Naturally, sending an email to the team won't grab your attention and interest the way creating a piece of artwork or an advertising campaign for a cause that you are passionate about. Therefore, set your goals with these guidelines with these criteria in mind. However, it is don't make it the only requirement for each objective. This can add a sense of novelty to your thoughts and helps you to become more balanced at the very least.

It is crucial to break up a target into smaller goals. It is much easier to gauge and set a schedule to observe yourself working towards your goal. A large goal with no concrete steps to reach it can make procrastination and distraction are much easier.

Making smaller steps towards the deadline will make it much easier to stop for breaks to replenish your batteries or to earn small rewards en towards the huge payout.

What's stopping you from moving forward?

It's time for you to take care of the things that affect the level of your production. Begin by making an outline of the items that frequently impede you when trying to get things off your list of things to do. If you're only getting started with to-do lists, create an inventory of the things that cause you to be distracted at least two days per week frequently.

Distractions can consume the equivalent of an hour of your daily time. This can result in a major gap in the time you that you have set aside for being productive.

With a typical workday of two hours 7 days per week and 52 weeks a year, you're spending the equivalent of 57,512 days in a state of distraction (based the average U.S. Lifespan of 79 years). With a little effort, at a minimum, some of the time could be put to better use.

One of the most significant causes of distraction, impedes and hinders effective time management is the use of social media. Being able to connect with others in the team via various channels of communication could be advantageous. The ability to do research in the field is clearly more beneficial than sitting in libraries for hours or even days only to discover that the idea you're researching isn't as good. However, the drawback of these obvious advantages is the accessibility to items you might have been living without.

There's no reason to check in with your friends as well as old school acquaintances every day on Facebook. There is no need to be informed immediately by email or notification that you have been invited to play on any of a social media platform.

To be honest nobody needs to to go through their emails every few minutes. Sure, crucial business transactions are completed through emailing documents. Negotiations can be conducted by email too. But for the vast most of us, checking our email each two-minute interval or every jingle is slowing down the progress we can build towards the finalization of the project in front of us or the concept that is gradually forming in an idea-making session.

Natural Tendencies and. "The How Everyone Does It"

Are you aware that you complete things much more easily in the morning or evening? Make the time needed for these tasks at times in the time you are most likely to succeed at completing them. Some people are not suited for an 8-to-5 workday or even to be successful during the daylight hours. If you are prone to having more inspiration or greater ambition during the afternoon or in the evening do not try to push yourself to be more productive early in the day. It won't work for you.

Make sure you plan your schedule so that you can achieve success. If you realize that you're slow to start in the morning, but then tend to get going in the afternoon, create your to-do-list with simpler tasks to complete in the morning and most of your work scheduled for completion in the afternoon.

Discovering your strengths is essential to be successful in many ways. Being aware of what you are enthusiastic about and are particularly skilled in opens the door to success, as does being efficient and organized. Explore the possibilities to figure out the most effective ways to approach an assignment or areas of the task that you are certain you excel at. Your next task is to be sure you place more emphasis on what you are proficient in, but also allow for more time for areas that you think are not in your area of expertise.

Chapter 10: Time Management

What exactly is time management and what can be utilized to propel you to discipline, action, productivity and success? Let's share a an example to demonstrate the concept of time management in a compelling way.

The professor has brought three containers of pebbles, big stones, as well as sand for the class. He requests a student to take the three trays and empty them into an empty bucket. A student comes towards the back of the classroom and begins working hard. He starts with sand, and then the pebbles, and then tries to take the rocks out. But, to his dismay, he's not able to put everything into the bucket.

The professor then looked over to the class and declared that was the only student who had filled the bucket with rocks at first followed by pebbles, and finally sand. could have fit everything inside.

This is exactly how time management functions. It's about organizing your pebbles, rocks and sand so that you can be able to fit everything into an incredibly small bucket, which is available all hours of the day. Concentrate on the most difficult and most significant tasks first, and then smaller, medium-sized tasks. If we concentrate on tasks that are smaller it is easy to be more obsessed about it than necessary. In our desire for perfectionism and over-analysis we can spend more time than is necessary on it. This can mean that we don't have enough time for larger and more hefty tasks.

In essence, the idea of managing time is planning, organizing and scheduling the time you have available to maximize your productivity. If you do not reserve enough time for the huge rocks, pebbles and sand could take up the entire time.

Time is the true value because when it's gone, it's impossible to be reclaimed. It is impossible to reverse the clock regardless of how much you wish to alter the course of. Every person has the same amount of time in a day (unless you're blessed with an undiscovered gadget (or superpower)). But, some individuals are able to accomplish many things on their own while others complain that they have no enough time to do things.

What is the reason that certain people are always able to finish their tasks in time, while others struggle to make time for both leisure and work? What makes some people can't only finish their tasks punctually but also have fun doing what they love while others are unable to meet deadlines?

Why are some people constantly taking their time and others are in a trance, like unrestrained chickens, trying finish tasks in the nick of time? It's all about time management. How you make the most of your time throughout the day will make a huge difference in your efficiency and productivity.

Here are a few of the most efficient strategies for managing time that can increase your productivity.

1. Set up a routine in the morning. This isn't a lie, however the way you start the day determines to a great extent how productive and useful you are during the course of your day. It's going to establish or set the tone for how much you'll accomplish in the day.

Beware of snoozing. Even if you're tempted to hit the snooze switch to get an extra few minutes of rest Get up and move. If you stay in bed, you feel tired and tired as well as you could get snoozed repeatedly. It's more difficult to wake up when alarms go off.

Begin with some exercise to feel rejuvenated and refreshed. This will stimulate your brain's activity area and improve your metabolism. Even a quick run or even on-the-spot exercises can help. Take advantage of the routine you have in your early morning and determine the pace of the rest of your day. I would highly suggest waking up early, before the other people in your home wake up. This could be the most efficient and most productive moment to work on your tasks.

It's also a good time to plan your day's events or to practice yoga/meditation. Respond to emails or make an action plan for the day prior to when it starts. If you're strapped to time and have a lot of work to do for the day, you must get organized. Create a well-planned and organized schedule by focusing your effort and focus on the most important and urgent tasks to be completed during the day. Prioritize tasks from to-do lists, and then plan your time around them.

Choose the three main things to do in the course of the day. What do you'd like to complete at the time the day is over? Prioritize these tasks. Anything else is a secondary concern. Do not try to do more than you are capable of handling in the course of your day. You'll be amazed by how much you can accomplish in your time management with this one trick.

2. Find and eliminate time-suckers. Try this short exercise to see where the majority of your time being spent. I call it an audit of your time every day. Conduct a 7-day review of how you are using your time. Keep track of everything in a phone or notebook. What do you have to be doing at the moment? Break it down into blocks of 30, 60, or 30 minutes. Did you get lots of things accomplished today? Was your time well-spent?

Have you wasted time or engaged in useless activities? If you're employing the four-quadrant approach to categorize your work, do so by your four quadrants. At the end of every week, add all of your data. Which area did you devote most or time? In which quadrant did most of your activities fall into? Your results might surprise you! We often believe that we are productive, but we're not. We are convinced that we're getting lots of things done due to multitasking. But the brain's performance and effectiveness are impacted when we are doing more than one thing at a time. Are you getting the results you want in efficiency and productivity, or just having too many things to complete.

The most destructive habits are time-wasters that are designed to lower productivity. The most disastrous thing about the time-wasters is that they provide us with feeling like we have accomplished many things. For instance, we can spend hours, telling ourselves that we are searching for ideas or researching. What is the point of use of our time online on Instagram,

Facebook or Pinterest for hours trying to find ideas? Instead, take a short look through the various sites and then go back to working.

Set a timer when needed. This method works for me. When I'm tempted to do some research or look for ideas online during my working hours, I schedule my social media and internet browsing. Set an alarm clock for the next 5-10 mins. If it sounds and you're from your surfing or brainstorming time before getting back on track. Also, you should time yourself when talking via the phone.

One of the most time-consuming activities I've realised is keeping track of and responding to emails all day. Our email inbox is always busy throughout the day, and we're enticed to read and respond to every email we receive during the course of doing other things, which can stifle the focus of the work in front of us. Beware of this. Instead, set aside the time to check and responding to emails (unless it's urgent). Be sure to ask yourself if what you're putting your time into adds any benefit to your work or efficiency.

Social media browsing, playing endless virtual games, binge-watching shows and other activities are all bad habits and time-wasters that drain your time and productivity. Make the most of your time in order to achieve your goals. The primary distinction between winners and losers is that the former can put off satisfaction and focus on the work that needs to be accomplished while keeping their eyes fixed on the larger perspective. They focus on the long-term rewards that drive them towards their goals through the best use of precious time resources. They are not often focused on the pleasures of instantaneous life.

We all admire the wealthy and successful, but we can't be a part of their struggles or the difficulties they encounter as well as the sacrifices they have to make to achieve a certain level of personal success. In addition to the other factors that make them successful includes the ability to manage time, delay reward, self-control, the ability to beat procrastination, and many more. We often wonder why we're not like the successful people whom we admire. Are you ready to let go of your time-wasting and unproductive habits? Are you willing to put off the gratification of others? Are you ready to be efficient and always striving to maximize your precious time resources? Are you able to your mind to put off short-term satisfaction for the long-term success? Make the most of your time in order to succeed.

It is not possible to get much accomplished by sitting and just watching Netflix for hours or playing virtual games unless you're an author, filmmaker or scriptwriter. games creator or writer. Make every minute a goal to increase your efficiency. This could speed up your path to success. It's true that things can become somewhat daunting at times. If you start to feel overwhelmed or overwhelmed by the work ahead Take a break or a power to sleep. Recollect your thoughts and return to work with renewed enthusiasm and energy.

If you've read the author Charles Duhig's work titled The Power of Habit, it describes keystone behaviors that connect all the other stones. These keystone habits don't just assist us in developing more productive habits, but they can also assist in removing ineffective routines. When we focus on keystone behaviors that help us effectively manage our time and make the process of creating habits that are related to time management productivity, procrastination, and time management easy.

Develop the brain's second side, too. For instance, devote time learning about skills that are out of your comfort zone or that you wouldn't think of doing. If, for instance, you're a doctor take some time to relieve the tension by learning to dance. A pianist, for instance, could learn Taekwondo. Engage in activities that go beyond your comfort zone in order to train your brain to learn new abilities.

3. Find some inspiration when you're not feeling inspired. Check out LinkedIn, YouTube, or Ted Talks every

time you feel your motivation to complete tasks slipping. These are great resources to help you get back on track with your inspiration. It's difficult to accomplish things when the desire from inside is exhausting. Find ways to turn on your passion by focusing on inspirational content and looking for motivation. Learning about successful people's experiences and their actions can get you back in action by activating the fire inside you.

I enjoy the idea of having an instructor who will help you stay on track, hold you accountable, and keep you focused on your goals. It's pretty easy to become lost and disengaged in the absence of someone to help you. However, when we are able to depend on someone else's guidance (who themselves have gone through the grind) and we can be more active and accountable. This keeps us motivated and motivated to keep on the right path. Find a mentor that can keep you focused on your goals and objectives.

4. Get the most out of that waiting period. Make the most of your waiting

time. There is lots of time to wait which can be utilized to increase productivity and maximize the time we have. For instance, in the terminal, in the coffee shop , waiting for the order to be taken, in the doctor's office and so on. Utilize the waiting time to complete smaller tasks such as sketching out a rough outline for an idea and brainstorming, imagining and scheduling activities for the following day as well as sending emails and messages and the list goes on. It's impossible to complete many difficult and intense tasks in this time. It's best to select a less demanding tasks that will take up a significant portion of your "doing" time. There's plenty of groundwork you can accomplish in the smallest of time gaps. We all know that the foundation is what creates the creation of a sturdy foundation.

5. Create a to-do list of things according to four quadrants. When you have completed each task, write the task on the list. This will provide you with a sense of satisfaction, accomplishment and satisfaction of having completed each task. This will inspire you to tackle more projects.

Use your downtime judiciously. There's plenty of filler or downtime time throughout the day, which can be utilized for creating your task lists. Why not use your travel time to plan, schedule and arranging the day's activities? It can also be utilized to listen to podcasts or audio books.

Don't spend every minute of your spare time to planning and organizing your day, as this could hinder productivity or time control. If you've got about 15 spare minutes, you should allocate five minutes to organising the daily tasks.

Take advantage of your weekends as well. This is me sounding like a dreaded productivity beast. You'll be amazed by how much you get done making the most of your weekends. There's a meme that circulates on social media of the man who throws papers into the air on a Friday night and then saying, "-- you are on the Friday." The following image shows the same man taking papers thrown in the air in the evening of Friday, and then at the beginning of Monday. It's pretty powerful, if you are me! A little planning and starting work during weekends can ease stress of the week ahead. It could be that is as simple as writing an outline or planning your entire week.

Spend about 2-4 hours each day working on tasks that are productive during the weekend. You'll have plenty of time to relax and recreation on weekends. Consider incorporating tasks into weekends and filler times throughout the day. You'll be amazed at how much you be able to accomplish.

Many of the most successful people organize their entire week one day prior to when the week begins. They stay focussed on their goals, and allows them to smoothly transition into the week ahead. When you are in an unwinding weekend routine it can be difficult to switch to more productive Monday. The transition is more smooth and less jerky by starting on Sunday.

The ability to start your day with a clearly defined plan can help you stay focused on the most important things. It is easy to change from a relaxed and relaxed mindset on the weekend to a focused Monday morning brain if prepare everything Sunday. Spend just a few minutes on Sunday to create plans for the entire week. Reduce the urge to delay by breaking down the weekly goals into tasks for each day to ensure that each time you have to complete something all you need to do is look at your list of tasks.

Be aware that your enthusiasm, energy and creative energy fluctuate throughout the course of. Set up low-effort and important tasks for Mondays or other days when your motivation and enthusiasm are at a low level. Also, plan the most demanding, creative and difficult tasks on Wednesday and Tuesday when your performance is believed as being at best. Set up meetings and brainstorming sessions on Thursdays when your team's performance begins to decline. Make use of Fridays to network and a recap of the week , and making plans.

6. Set up regular reminders. If you don't want to be behind schedule and

maximize your time, schedule regular reminders of alarms, deadline alerts and alarms on your devices at regular intervals rather than the last deadline. Making reminders on a regular basis for deadlines that are sub-deadlines will help you stay on the right track to meet the deadline to meet, rather than waiting until the very last minute.

For example, if you are working on a project to be completed in the next four weeks, schedule reminders not just the final day of the 28-day period, but as well on the days of 7, 12 18, 24, and 28. This will ensure that you're in the right direction in the steps required to complete the task. You will be reminded regularly of the assignment, and staying in the right direction instead of running about trying to complete the task at the very of the deadline.

7. Get up early. Have you ever heard that many of the most successful individuals belong to that 5 a.m. group? Here you are, asleep in awe and wondering how you won't be able to achieve the success and wealth

they enjoy. It's about discipline, time management and the ability to make a. You decide what you do which will ultimately affect the likelihood of your being successful.

If you ask me about my most preferred time management method is to get up early and getting started as quickly as is possible. It can give you an advantage unlike other methods. The famous quote of Mark Twain is worth noting here. He wrote, "If it is your task to consume a frog it is recommended to start it early to get up in the morning. If it's your responsibility to feed two frogs it is recommended to consume the larger one first." This basically summarizes the essence of ace techniques for time management.

If you are scared of having to do a lot within one day, get started at a reasonable time. Make sure that everything you need for the task in order prior to night to avoid the time-wasters like trying to determine how to begin.

Let's say, for instance, suppose you're making a critical report based on the information and data that you've collected over time. Be sure to keep all your research properly organized in a file or document that is easy to access. If you have everything that you need to start, it's easy to go into action mode and then pick up speed.

If you spend time trying to determine the best place to start it will slow the process of beginning and finishing the job. In the previous example If all your information and figures are readily available to you, it's simpler to start.

Also, if you've got an important meeting or presentation scheduled for the following day, make sure you have your outfit and all other things prepared the day before so that you don't lose time or spend your time trying to locate items. A large portion of our mornings are spent deciding how to dress and planning out our outfit to wear for our day. If you have everything prepared prior to the day it's much easier to concentrate on the important job at hand.

If you've got lots of tasks planned to do in the coming day and they're all important, you should tackle the most difficult task first. It is important to complete the most lengthy and challenging job (remember the professor's sand, pebbles , and rock examples?) before noon. After you've completed an overwhelming task, you'll feel more satisfaction. This will encourage you to take on the next tasks with a more determined and action-oriented mindset.

If you are certain that you will have plenty of time to complete the following day or have a lengthy workday ahead, try to be sure to avoid staying up midnight. Few things can hinder productivity and time management more greater than sleep deprivation. Get up early and get uninterrupted sleep for 8-9 hours awake, fresh and energized for the next day. A lack of sleep can leave you tired, depleted of energy, and difficult to concentrate (low in concentration and mental alertness).

One of the most detrimental ways to reduce your productivity and time management goals is to begin the day without any ideas of where to start. Imagine spending just half an hour trying to determine the best place to start or what should be accomplished throughout the day. This time could have been used to get started on your day's work and end early. Then you'll be completing the task in the evening, which does not give you enough time to plan the day's schedule. You're caught in a vicious cycle. Beware of rushing from one task to anotherand wasting time. Make a plan for your day ahead of time , so you can boost your productivity.

Always suggest clearing your desk from the previous day and creating an agenda of the tasks that have to be accomplished the following day. This is called the decompression technique. It will give you a feeling of happiness, renewal and a sense of freshness when you enter a neater clean, organized and better appearance desk. Be a bit early to work and begin making the materials that you require to start your day off with an erupting start. This tip can be the only factor that affects your work efficiency throughout the day.

8. Utilize time, work and abilities. Have you ever wondered why certain people achieve remarkable outcomes while others just slog out despite the fact that everyone is working the same 24 hours per day? It's all about doing smart work and making the best use of time through leveraging efforts, time and abilities.

For instance, you work all day long and only 12-15 hours are available to pursue productive activities. If you are working even 15 hours per day, for five days in every week, you're clocking productive time of up to 75 hours, and likely overworking yourself.

Then, consider using the time, effort, and skills. Three people are hired who each contribute 40 hours of their time each week, which is 120 hours in a week! Notice the difference? Running a marathon can limit your potential to grow. There's only a certain amount you can do by yourself.

But, if you're running relays, there's plenty you can accomplish. Through leveraging other people's efforts, time and energy it's not exhausting yourself. Everyone contributes small amounts to help contribute to overall productivity, instead of the one person who is trying to do everything. The most successful individuals around the globe recognize the importance of using time, knowledge, and efforts. They build empires based on the efforts of others, their time and talents.

Outsource or delegate time-consuming jobs. Remember the 80-20 rule of Pareto? The only 20 percent of your efforts are responsible for 80 percent of your outcomes. What's the reason you would want to spend the rest of your time doing nothing different? Do you not want to improve your performance by investing more time into your work that is clearly benefitting you? Transfer tasks and responsibilities that take up a large portion of time. It's not easy at the beginning to find another person to complete your job. If you don't educate people and assign the responsibilities, you'll be running the race by yourself and limit your success. The process of outsourcing and delegating work is a smart way to cut down on time. It helps reduce your workload and allows you to concentrate on the tasks that produce results. By focusing your attention on a particular task you're preventing the brain's speed from reducing. We've all heard that multitasking is not a good idea. In order to increase your productivity and make your life more efficient, you should spend your time on things that yield outcomes while delegating more time-consuming tasks to other people. It is possible to delegate tasks to team members by educating and guiding them, or employ skilled and knowledgeable freelancers. Employing people from the home could require some time and effort to train them but it is worthwhile over the long run.

9. Establish your routine. This is something that is easy to do, yet it's surprising that so many people do not follow it. It is more likely that you will make more of the time you have when you stick to a set routine. If you don't have a set time set for the activities of

your daytime, then you'll be losing a lot of your time due to having no control over your time. Create a schedule that is clear for your day's activities. This will help that you have all the resources to complete your tasks. Plan each day like you're organizing an important event.

These are the most efficient time management techniques to put you in high productivity, reduce waste of time, and organize your available time resources , and snap off of snooze mode.

Chapter 11: Correlation Between Time Management Skills and Success

When we start this chapter, I'd like warn you. We've seen the many clichés of putting ourselves into others' shoes. This is an instance you shouldn't do it. Do not look at an individual who appears to be successful and say that you'd like to be like them. You're not sure what they sacrificed to achieve such success. Someone could be looking at you and saying that he would prefer if there was the family he has now. Are we crystal in the right direction? Take a take a look at your life and decide what you would like to achieve in accordance with your needs and priorities.

What is success? Success' definition is contingent on the person you ask. My concept of success concerns predominantly with family and the world generally. Others' definition of success is dependent on the success of a particular career and that's it. Therefore, let's examine the true definition and look at what it means. The actual definition is "the positive or successful conclusion of endeavors or attempts that result in the attainment of objectives; the achievement of wealth, status and honours or similar." We have it. With this definition at heart, people who think of it as something that is a familial or life event, like me and those who think of it as a job thing, both are correct. It is all dependent on your goals and beliefs.

In order to make a case for argument's sake, let's suppose that success is related to your professional career. Your focus is on work and you'd like to achieve as much success with your career as you possibly can. You're looking to learn the best way to utilize time management to achieve this target. Let's take a look at some strategies to achieve this. Be aware that this is focusing upon "human-doing" the task of managing your time.

Let me start by saying this. Always keep in mind to work in a way that is smart and not overly too hard. Work harder, does not mean that you're more efficient. It is possible to be a tad grumpy and not accomplish anything. It happens frequently. Anyone who falls into this group are easily trapped in this cycle of non-productive and hard work. Make sure you are smart about your work and make smart decisions about time management. Keep this in your mind: time is the only thing that's identical for everyone. No regardless of how much you've got you aren't able to purchase more. The same time span is available to everyone, and has the same starting and ending for everyone of us. The ones who succeed never forget these two facts. They think strategically and are aware of the fact that time isn't refundable.

Dale Beaumont, the founder of Business Blueprint, has a handful of seminars on time management accessible on the internet. On one of his YouTube videos the speaker discusses time management and offers an example. When I saw him speak I was reminded of my own time-saving technique of brushing my teeth while doing other chores, however, the topic was business related. He suggested using the time spent in the car to be an opportunity to plan. He also mentioned Parkinson's Law which is the idea that work grows to make up time to finish it. If you're in need of more explanation of this then it's that you should know that your work tasks will come up with a method to be completed until you allow them to. This can have both positive and negative aspects and depends on the way you decide to utilize it.

The initial suggestion for using time management to build an excellent career is to make a plan for your day, and never start the day before the planning is completed. The ideal time to plan should be during the day or evening in the evening, possibly while you spend time with your spouse. However, it has to be kept secret. Plan your day ahead. Plan your week ahead. Plan your year ahead. The more you plan the more efficient. Let's say your day is set. Now is the time to head to work. Let's look at the ways we can increase our results.

It is likely that your decision to pursue a career is based largely on your capabilities and strengths. Most people do not pick an occupation that's most difficult however, if they pick that option, it usually does not last for long. Therefore, you've got an understanding of the things you excel at and what you might not be great at. It doesn't stop at the start of your professional career. It should be considered into any decisions that have a bearing on your career. This is a second clever example. What can you do? It's simple. When you can, delegate the work that is more difficult or time-consuming for someone who is able to finish it quicker and with less effort. In this instance, you must determine the cost-benefit ratio. You must ensure that the extra cost is justified and proves that they are more useful to the overall goal or project.

Another suggestion for success that relates to smart work is to look at hiring experts in specific areas to either help you when needed , or show you how to get better in the particular area. If you think hiring an instructor can make you more productive over the long term the cost will likely to be worth it. Additionally, it can help with managing your time. You'll spend less time doing something else, which allows that time to be allocated to another. A good illustration of what I'm speaking of is the accountant who hires tax preparers for the period of February through April to complete tax returns for these customers , giving the accountant the time to tackle more complicated situations. This saves not only the accountant's time, but also cash since tax preparers earn less than accountants. This means that the cost of overhead for each billable hour is reduced. The productivity is improved as is the cost reduced. It's a win-win-win for any company I know of.

The delegation of tasks, giving the responsibility and obligations to another person, as well as sub-contracting on a temporary or permanent basis is essential for the development and growth of any company. This goes beyond managing time. This is common sense. If it's not common sense that's certainly not. If you looked at the agenda of the most highly successful executives, I'm pretty sure you'd be amazed by the number of specific responsibilities the CEO has. The most successful people are characterized in their capacity to delegate, and perform it efficiently possible.

Another strategy for success is to make use of what is called forced deadlines. It is important to note that this is an area that is easy to mess things up. We'll discuss it later, but today I'm referring to one of the most obnoxious curse words in the business world that is procrastination. It's easy to put things off in the event that you're not cautious and aren't experienced in business. The most effective way to fight the urge to delay is to make deadlines as they force our brains to be in a constant state of mind. This lets us imagine finish lines in which we must be in the lead of the pack and don't just appear near the final stage of the day, but spread throughout.

Deadlines will force you to look at things in a more efficient way. You'll be able to work faster moving forward quickly and easily and have confidence boosted. You could also test you to be at a higher standard. What's the difference between scheduled deadline and a normal deadline? I'm not sure. It's available in a different book. Of course, it's an amusing joke, but we wanted to make sure you're still paying close attention. In reality, it's an apple that is large apple and a very big apple. When you have a deadline that is forced the end or deadline is set with the aim of making it easier or increase the efficiency of the task. You plan to alter the course of the job and making it more efficient or faster.

Okay. We've examined the idea of using unproductive time outsourcing, delegating work and sub-contracting, as well as training and deadlines and other suggestions for successful time management. Nowlet's take a look at some other ideas and suggestions offered by people with experience and proved their strategies successful. I would like to remind you once again that the very first step, and most crucial aspect of managing your time is knowing what you intend to achieve by using your time, and remember that time is indestructible and cannot be refunded. It is only available once, so choose what you believe is right for you at the time. This is an area of life that you must be yourself and make decisions by what you'd like to do rather than what other people might wish to see from you. When you reach time's end in your journey you are the one that will be the ones to blame when you fail to do this.

In this section, I'm going take another personal experience to illustrate time management. In the past, I wrote about my priority being with my family more than work and the way that this conviction led me to quit the general management position at the chain of a rent-to-own and retail store. This is a different example of my experience with the same company, and in the same job where I learned some things while there. The most efficient and time-savvy business owners understand the importance of staffing. they select employees who can and are willing to perform all tasks required of them and tasks assigned to them, regardless of whether the tasks are routine or fall within what is included in their job description. If you're instructed by your boss to complete something, you have to perform it or think about looking for a new job. Management must be aware that when given tasks or other responsibilities you'll perform your work in addition to it and complete the task in a timely, efficient and totally. They want you to be able to do this without being directed throughout the process and without having to be watched. If you're not relied upon by the management, then you're likely to have only a few years with that business.

The store in which I was employed was franchisee. Corporate had a precise and clear personnel model, and also guidelines that was based on the number of customers that particular store. The more customers the store served and the higher employees it would require. As the manager in charge was able to hire and remove any employee at any time. Therefore, if I did not believe the employee's performance was performing up to standard, I was able to take action. I was not able to blame any other person for an employee who did harm to business , other than me since I had the power to rectify the issue. The issue with that was it was a long and complicated procedure when it came to bringing in and training someone and often it seemed as if it was simpler to simply forgive an employee for their inefficiency and productivity.

The company I worked for consisted of several stores. My franchise was comprised of about 40 stores. Everything that occurred in my store was on me and I was accountable. I was rewarded when the store did very well. When there was a problem with my store or on a downslope in business, I was required to be accountable for it. In actual this was the reason that determined the length of my tenure. There was a weekly evaluation of all stores across every area. If your shop remained on most prominent position on the chart, then you can rest assured that your work was in good hands at the moment. My store was always in the top spot and I planned on maintaining it at that level. While my main priority was and will always be my children, I did everything I could to do my best at work. All of this culminated after a couple of months of my tenure there.

I was of the opinion that it was more troublesome hiring a new employee rather than ignore issues with employees. I was aware that regardless of whether the employee was good or not I was accountable and accountable for all that was happening to my business. And, not only that, my earnings were directly tied to the financial success of the shop. Thus I had no option but to ensure that the store I owned was as profitable and efficient as I could. And, at the end of the day my bottom line would be what my management could be able to see. The other information I wanted to keep inside the office. This includes staffing and every employee's performance.

There was a worker who was quite smart, but the way he used that intelligence was in ways that weren't the most effective. He knew for a fact that no matter if he performed lots of work or just the minimum job required to stay in his job, his salary would be the same. He also knew that I did not often terminate employees due to the difficulties hiring and training a new. In addition, he was aware that I had not the time to to ensure that the person was actually working. What happened was that he didn't perform any work, at all. This is not exaggerated out of the proportions. He was an awful employee and I did the most horrible choice I could have made and completely blew my time management skills to pieces. I was tempted to take on his work, and my own, in his place. This was a huge error, and I soon was entangled in a cycle of working extremely hard and producing very little. Then, he was let go and another person was hired to fill his spot. Things were much better by this point and I pledged to never reach that point again. The point I'm trying to bring out here is to not delay things or avoid doing due to the difficulties. If it's efficient for your company it is the recommended to take it on. The majority of managerial decisions like this one deals in some way with managing time.

There are many aspects of time management to talk about and plenty of examples to be utilized, but I do not want to waste your time and neither do I wish to spend my time in a rambling. This chapter focuses on taking actions with respect to time management which can improve your business's efficiency and productivity. I believe we have adequately discussed this. This is a brief summary of the topics we've discussed.

The most important items to keep in mind are the items that you consider to be your top priorities. Your time management should be in line with your values and beliefs. After that, you are able to move to the next stage. Begin planning your day ahead, and do not start your day until your planning is completed. Examine the areas of your inactive time and think about how you can incorporate things like planning to make the most of your time. When you plan your work you can delegate or outsource whenever it is appropriate. It is also possible to outsource when it improves productivity and reduce time. Select your staff carefully and don't delay completing a task due to the fact that it could be an arduous or time-consuming task. It is better to complete the task and completed. Make goals and establish priorities. Let yourself learn from those who are more skilled or knowledgeable in specific areas. Reread this chapter and the book as often as is necessary to retain the majority of the lessons you learned studying it.

The last thing to be mentioned in this chapter is the common thread between successful individuals and their personality. Similar to every other component of a business that is successful there must be some element of assertiveness. People who are assertive tend to be better at business for example. They are steadfast and steadfast in their beliefs. They are able to declare no, and they aren't easily diverted from their route. The ones that are assertive tend to be leaders instead of followers. This is as true when it comes to time management, as it is in the other aspects of the business. When you plan, it is important to establish clearly defined goals, stay focused on the goal you are seeking, and willing to do whatever it takes to get it. These qualities are essential to success and a successful plan. The ability to assert yourself can be taught or developed. If you're not confident now, try becoming more assertive. This will be extremely helpful in managing your time.

Chapter 12: to Do-list apps

Technology has altered how we conduct many things, including the way we manage our time. One could say that technology has depleted our time resources, as we are constantly looking at our Facebook pages, scrolling through Twitter and browsing Instagram but to no efficient end. We also spend way too often looking at our email, even though doing it less frequently would be acceptable too!

Technology has simplified many aspects to our advantage. There are a lot of to-do list and time management applications available, which will help you to be more productive. Some people prefer doing things online however it's something worth considering. Let's look at the two.

The Old-Fashioned Style or let Technology Aid?

If you're not sure about which route to go, let's examine the two options and find out which is the best choice with the most pros and cons in each direction.

Utilizing a Time Management Application

Apps available on the market could be a literal to-do lists that you manage yourself or have many different options to utilize including alarms, reminders, notes, and adjustments guidelines. There are no-cost versions, but there are those that cost money depending on the amount of usage you will get from the application to determine if you'd be willing to pay for it or not.

The advantages of using an app

You can access your application wherever you are, so if you're sitting in the back of a bus, or strolling down the street, you'll be able to track your progress in that particular week or day

Add items to your wish list quickly and effortlessly

Your app could have other options, like reminders and tools that can help you stay on the right track

*There's a variety of apps available for both paid and free and you can choose the most suitable app by looking around and comparing

Readjusting your list of things to do whenever a new task comes in is much more simple and less messy if you use an application

Pros and Cons of using an app

If your smartphone is taken or lost, or when it is damaged and you're not able to access your phone's app, and, consequently, your list of apps.

You are the sole judge of the battery in your phone!

Some people like the feeling of ticking or crossing off an item on a piece piece of paper

Certain apps may be difficult to comprehend initially and could include many more functions than what you require.

Utilizing Traditional Methods
Traditional Method

When we say "traditional method," we mean the use of a notebook or paper along with a pencil or pen. You could write an outline and mark items off while you work, or you can draw your table and tailor it according to your requirements.

Benefits of using an Old Method

* You will be able to clearly see before you what you must do.

A lot of people enjoy the feeling of marking off things physically, because it gives an incredible sense of satisfaction and excitement

* You can make things easier to cross out quickly

It's a far simpler format that can be used by anyone who wants to utilize

Pros and Cons of Using a Traditional Method

You could erase your list and you'd be in a mess!

If you need to alter and change things around, your checklist could become quite messy and difficult to read or comprehend.

You're missing out on the extra features included with the application

Finding a particular format can be difficult when writing out an outline, e.g. columns

How to use a Pen and Paper Format

For you to get a complete outline of the best kind of list to make for you, we're going to be quick to explain how to make use of the format of paper for a to-do list. It's an easy task however, to make the most of this particular kind of checklist, you'll need to think of several various options.

If you're not planning to use technology in this case, you'll need to get notebooks in which you make notes. If you've got a single piece of paper or post-it notepad laying around in your home, you're more likely to be able to lose it, which could be a minor calamity. It's much easier to stick to your plan and keep it in use in a convenient and relaxing place to keep it all in. Make sure you choose the right notebook with an elastic loop to hold pencils or pens so that you're not looking for a pen that has gone missing!

If you are looking for a basic home to-do list, a simple flip-book would suffice to easily carry it around in pockets or carry in your bag. For a business list it is recommended to choose an A5-sized version that has a hardback alternative. It is that is easier to write on. You may be asking yourself what it is you are supposed to be thinking about the details that you write in, but when are looking to make the most of the situation and help you to make your life easier to write in, these little details can have a major impact.

For a basic home to-do list, you simply need to make a page each day. You will note down every task you have to complete each day, and then tick each one off when you're going. The aspect of priority isn't that important in order to maximize your time, get up in the morning and create your list, and then number the tasks from 1 to whatever in the order you plan to accomplish them, one being the most crucial.

To create the A5 style of to-do-list, you can make columns inside your notebook or note everything down in a list format. Each week, you should have a page and perhaps flip the page in a landscape orientation and be sure to add a include a date each time the tasks are added to your list. This will allow you to see how long ago tasks have been. Write down the task, the importance it is, then mark it off as you move along.

The traditional method is definitely the most efficient method however it is not able to include the singing, dancing, and the beneficial characteristics of apps.

Best To Do List Apps

We've discussed the traditional approach versus a technological approach; now we have to provide some insight into the most effective applications for managing time currently available. The options are vast however we've chosen a few of the top ones, based on user-friendliness features, functionality, and general capacity to produce.

Google Keep

It's definitely one of the most effective to-do lists available and the best part is that it's completely free available on Android as well as iOS! The interface is easy and simple to use and although it comes with additional features, like the ability to include notes written and voice-over photos and putting your tasks into categories they are easy to implement and won't give the user a headache when trying to get your hands on the application! It also lets you invite others for tasks that you add to your list (useful for collaboration at work). It's not just necessary to create a list of tasks here, you can also add an itemized shopping list in conjunction with your main list!

The only downside that is typical of this particular application is that a lot of users were not a fan of the alarm or reminder system However, the simplicity of the app makes it a good option for those who are just beginning their journey.

Todoist

This is among the most complete to-do list applications you can find on the market and for that reason, you'll need to purchase it. It won't make you rich however, since paying for the premium version costs about $30 per year at present. The free version gives you enough space to complete simple task-based planning, and could be enough all-around.

This particular application allows you to connect it with the accounts on your social networks for quick sign-in and setting it up is a breeze. You can add tasks at any point, and assign priority and deadlines to mark the most important tasks quickly and easily. When it comes to completing your tasks, just mark a box and you'll feel a sense satisfaction as you accomplish this!

The best features, which that you pay for, include reminders, additional comments and an automated backup system to ensure you won't lose any important information.

Evernote

Evernote is an extremely popular choice to take notes however, you can also make use of its time management tools to make a great to-do list. It lets you note notes, create reminders, voice memos and even photographs, and you can include additional documents if you want to, such as ones that are created using Word and PDFs. When you add items in your to-do list, it'll be synced between all your devices which means you don't have to be concerned about updating all of it more than once in the event that you've installed the app on both your tablet and smartphone, for instance.

Free versions are plenty for regular users However, it is possible to upgrade your account a premium account for a minimal cost of $35 to $70 per year at present, based on the plan you choose to purchase. There are many additional features available for paid accounts that include the ability add items to your list of items when you're offline or have additional storage. You can also add the option of a password security feature.

Wunderlist

Wunderlist is used for a long time as a no-cost version for those who don't require something too fancy or sophisticated or expensive, and require a simple and easy to use application that does what it's supposed to accomplish. This is how you can sum Wunderlist perfect.

You can also opt to use the free version or change to the more premium edition at a cost of around 60 dollars per year at present however there's a lot of features available in the free version which is why it's worthwhile to try it first to test the waters. This version allows you to make groups and also invite colleagues (up up to 25 people at a time) and having the ability to add notes and reminders on your list. The premium version offers additional features, including adding the notes as well as documents. For those looking to manage their home or work tasks The free version of Wunderlist is hard to beat.

Microsoft To Do

If you are a regular user of Microsoft Office, this particular application (free) is the perfect choice for syncing all your files. Due to the name of the company it is guaranteed to be of high the best, and that's exactly what you will get. The app was initially developed by Wanderlist but was later purchased by Microsoft and thus combines the top of both worlds. The way it functions is like the Wanderlist version as well which is an absolute plus.

It is easy to create tasks and put memos and reminders but there's another integrated feature, known as My Day. It allows you to make a daily calendar that can be used in conjunction with your main task list and then group them together. It's like taking the tasks on your primary daily or monthly list and assigning the tasks to a specific day, and then you're prioritizing them according to order. It's much more simple to do in reality than it is in the words!

Clear To-dos

Also, if you're looking for an app that is easy to use and does not add unnecessary clutter to your life Clear To-dos can be an ideal choice. However, the app isn't available for Android and you have to download it for iOS.

The layout of this application might be basic however it is elegant in the same way. It is possible to alter its appearance, e.g., background colors and fonts and font, etc. So you can make it easier to comprehend, while being stylish simultaneously! It is also possible to sync all your data to your Apple devices via this app as well as iCloud which means you're never lacking important data between devices.

The app is completely free up to an extent and after a specific number of hours of use the app will reach what's known as a "paywall. If you'd prefer to pay one time and be finished with the app, an alternative app might be better and for less frequent use every day this app is a good alternative.

These are the six top and most well-known to-do lists and time management software available. Make sure you review and modify your application whenever you feel it is appropriate your work style might not be static forever and you may need to alter your approach to a degree, as your work shifts or when demand increases.

If you're unsure whether to go to free versions or opt for the premium version This is something that only you are able to decide. The most effective option is to opt for an initial free version and then test the application to see how it performs. This will allow you to get an idea of whether it will work for you or not and if it works and you are satisfied enough to make use of the additional features, you might want to you should try the premium version for one month. If at the end of the month you aren't convinced it's worth the cost you are able to end your subscription (take a look at for the tiny print) and then try an alternative.

The best task list application is largely trial and trial and to try a few different options in your quest for the task management and organization!

DISTINGUISH between TIMEBOXING and the TIME CHUNKING METHODOLOGY

Timeboxing and the time-chunking method provide different ways of achieving similar objectives.

TIMEBOXING RUNS LONG before it was widespread. It's a method of limit the amount of time that is allocated to a certain project or task. When a timebox, the user assesses the progress made in the task that is in front of them, and asks the following question: "Does the work I've done meet the demands of the job?"

If yes, then no further work is done on the project or task. If no the time box is scheduled according to the need.

Timeboxing was initially developed to allow teams to manage their projects. The idea was to decrease the possibility that a project might extend beyond the scope of its project. This, in turn, aids the person or team to finish the project on time.

One of the advantages of using time-boxes in this way is that it keeps your body from being a victim of Parkinson's Law. This law states that "work increases to take up the time to complete it." In the event that you allocate 4 hours for an exercise, that activity is likely to take 4 hours to finish. If you are allotted 1 hour, you're probably to finish it in one hour.

Timeboxing allows you to set the time limit within the course of your task. By committing to the timeframe, it establishes an end date. It requires you to work towards the goal of completing the task instead of simply doing it. It also deters perfectionists.

Chapter 13: Timeboxing vs. Time

Chunking Method

The method of time-chunking is a form of timeboxing technique. As we mentioned at the start of this article it is recommended to do 25-minute chunks and then take 5-minute breaks in between each segment. (Again I highly recommend exploring different durations, and then creating the time chunking method in a way to complement your work flow and ability to concentrate.)

The time of a box can vary technically from a few minutes up to several months. It's dependent on the type of activity or project. This could be a series of hundreds of different tasks.

The idea behind time chunking is designed to help you stay focused. In Step 2.2, it was designed to ensure that the brain is able to focus for a short period of time. Once that time has passed it will require a short break.

Timeboxing was created to handle projects in a manner that the time doesn't get wasted on these projects. It also discourages perfectionists.

When you use the time-chunking technique allows you to be flexible to satisfy your desires for perfection. You can allocate any amount of time you want to an undertaking. There's no formal assessment process which requires you to review your progress and decide whether you've satisfied the project's specifications.

It's a big contrast from timeboxing. When you use timeboxing, you establish the deadline, for instance 2 hours - for each project. The deadline can be flexed. If, at the time it is due you aren't able to meet the requirements of the task, calculate the amount of time you'll need to dedicate to the task and add another time box. While the deadline may be flexible, it propels you to complete the task. It calms the perfectionist in you and makes it easier to concentrate only on "shipping."

It's an effective instrument to increase your efficiency. This raises the question...

Which one should you choose Which Method Should You Choose: Timeboxing or the Timing Chunking Method?

In a word, both.

Your productivity is influenced two factors:

1. your ability to concentrate upon the job at the moment

2. your capability to ship

The method of time-chunking helps you concentrate, but not your capacity for shipping (at least it's not direct). Timeboxing is a method to help you ship but not your capacity to concentrate (at at the very least it is it's not direct).

What is the reason to employ both strategies to tackle both issues simultaneously? Let's look at an illustration:

Imagine you're writing a lengthy blog article. Because of your experience with similar blogs previously you're aware that you could write the initial draft in just two hours. Begin by timeboxing. You will have 2 hours for the completion of the draft. Use the method of time chunking to divide that two-hour chunk into a number of work pieces.

If you're using a standard models of time-based chunking, the schedule would be as follows:

• Work out for 25 minutes

*Take 5 minutes to rest.

Work for 15 minutes

*Take five minutes to take a break

* Work for 25 minutes

*Relax for 5 minutes.

Work for 25 mins

*Take 15 minutes to rest

*Work for 20 minutes in order to finish the task

This is equivalent to 2 minutes of working.

Personally, I've used an altered model that adapted to my personal workflow. It could look similar to the following:

**Work out for 50 minutes

*Take an hour break

Work for an hour

* Take 10-minute breaks

Work for about 20 mins

*Take an 20-minute break

The key is that the time-chunking method is able to work in conjunction with timeboxing, allowing you to boost the daily output. Both methods are capable of adapting to each other.

Certain people believe in timeboxing and say they would not be able to perform their work any other way. Some people are adamant about the time chunking method and also make similar claims regarding its efficiency. There's no reason to pick between the two. Utilize both.

This guide is in fact focused on the time chunking method. This is why I'm not spending a huge amount of time to other methods of time management. However, it's worthwhile to mention timeboxing as a valuable addition to time chunks.

I would encourage you to test this method. Alongside being able to work within time chunks, create time boxes which restrict how much time you'll spend on tasks. You'll be amazed at how it can rid you of the perfectionism. This alone is an important step towards increasing your efficiency.

Chapter 14: How to Do When You First Start

Feeling overwhelmed

One thing you should be aware of is that everybody feels overwhelmed at some point in their professional and personal life. The organization of your life can help you be less overwhelmed, however there will be situations where you do not know how manage all the things you need to accomplish. There are some essential points you must keep in mind that you might not consider to be work-related, but they are a part of your performance at work and at home. You must follow the tips below, as it is crucial. Here are some tips you can employ to help you feel less overwhelmed

• Get a good quality sleep each night

* Try to turn off your work when you've planned your schedule for the day.

• Turn off your cell phone during the daytime hours.

* Learn to delegate

* Ensure that you are taking regular breaks

The most common reaction of those who are stressed is to do more than they can handle because they worry about how to keep up with their household and work obligations. If you stick to the four tips provided above, you're placing yourself in a good position and everything else is simple. Let's look at some things that could be difficult:

Your workload is excessive If you are juggling many responsibilities and you're an occasional perfectionist, it is likely that you are doing too much of the work by yourself. Learn to delegate and include others, both at home and on the job aspect. When you are able to trust your colleagues you are able to share the burden and still get the same level of success. One way to achieve this in the workplace is to delegate part of the workload to people who you think are capable of handling the job and ensuring you record a diary reminder to ensure that it's done. Review your list of tasks and determine the extent to which you are able to delegate, so that the list becomes easier to manage. Also, ensure that each item on your list is broken down into smaller pieces. Sometimes, you can delegate portions of the task to other people and then write an overview of the entire task once everyone has completed their share. The responsibility doesn't have to be completely on your shoulders. In fact, if you divide the work into smaller pieces and you can are in better control since it's much easier to finish small tasks instead of trying to complete a huge job by yourself.

At home, be open with your spouse about the work load that you're juggling. Ask your partner's assistance in doing those mundane tasks that have you feeling down. In a relationship you are able to do more things together, and if you're open about being overwhelmed Your partner will gladly offer assistance occasionally to assist you out with your obligations.

Review your job It is a requirement for everyone to perform this task every now and then, and If you have better ideas that you can do more Don't be afraid to schedule an appointment and discuss it with the boss. There could be certain company policies which are making you feel uneasy. It could, for example there are too many meetings consuming your time productively. If your boss can cut them down to just the essential ones, that gives you the time you need to complete everything that are on your list of things to be done promptly. If you notice that you're stifled with more tasks than you initially had this is actually a compliment as it indicates that your boss is trusting you, however, you have to inform him or her whether you need to add additional team members or experience in the fields that consume the majority amount of time.

Review your work load When you're overwhelmed, sit back and review the items you have to do. Do not stress about them. Just determine the priority of each item, as some have less importance than others. The problem is that those who are overwhelmed can look at all the tasks and get overwhelmed and panic. Take a deep breath and look objectively at the list, and then alter the priorities, getting these tasks out of the manner you can to reduce your list to a manageable size. Consider jobs are easy to delegate and transfer these. They can be addressed in the same manner, and with the same degree of urgency, however they do not necessarily have to be handled by you. Consider things that could be left until tomorrow. Take these items off your to-do list for today, since the simple of the fact that your list is long is what worries you. Be sure to add the items for tomorrow's list.

The most important thing to be certain of is that you're not adrift by thinking about things. Many people spend more time thinking about things than actually being productive. If you take a look at your list, make a decision on the priorities you want to achieve and delegate whenever it is possible the list will get smaller and easier to manage. This will allow you to tackle the task with more certainty that you can complete it. If you've never done it, you should take an unplanned break and don't bring your phone along. Find something that isn't at all related to work, and keep in mind that a break should be only that - an escape from everything. The reason why this is important is to allow you to return to work with a new outlook as well as less excuses. The short break, whether for coffee or lunch allows your mind to relax so that when it is time to return to the work to be completed that you can do it with a mindset that is capable of handling the task with less anxiety. Procrastination is a result of worry and procrastination causes being under-achieved. Therefore, try to beware of this. Pause and then go back to work in with full force.

The difference between feeling busy or being busy or

We often believe we're busy because of the amount we work. The more work that we must complete and complete, the busier we become. Also, the fewer tasks we are required to complete more relaxed as well as "lazier" we feel. We can be overwhelmed even though there's not much to do, or feel relaxed even in the midst of chaos. The state between "busy" as well as "not busy" aren't easily determined by the things we do and what we do or don't do. The brain is able to only do small things at a time. Being overwhelmed is more than just a mental state and, in general.

What's my top priority When I'm Feeling Overwhelmed?

Human beings are the sole creature living in nature who challenge the the status quo. We are all about having fun in the sun or travel to cities that never rest. However, natural ebbs, such as dark days between them and the period between seasons are both natural and essential. The message is simple If you feel tired, you should rest. Relax as nature would do during the midst of changes.

What If I don't have enough Time?

There's only so many hours that our bodies are able to function for before they begin to feel tired. As you get tired you make more errors you feel more exhausted, are more inclined to fight and you realize that you're not thinking as clearly as you could. This is the primary issue with time. Another issue is the fact that it is a finite resource and constantly decreasing each second. A lot of us don't have a lot of time to spend, and in trying to fill in additional time, we compromise sleeping.

However, sleep is extremely crucial. If you sleep for less than one hour can seriously reduce the cognitive capacity of our brains. Therefore, when you try to fill in more time without sleeping you compromise the effectiveness of your work and do greater harm than benefit for yourself. Therefore, don't try to manage the time better. Manage your energy.

Do I need to do everything by myself?

It's not a good idea. If you do all the work yourself, it makes it more difficult for you and hinders other people from taking part. Everyone deserves a opportunity to shine. Give yourself more time at work and home and make time to do the things you love doing.

What do you need to know to convince me to say no?

A lot of people say that they accept requests from strangers since they don't wish to let their colleagues down. But, it may be more about not being able to let others down, and also to feel valued. If we take a look inside ourselves we will like others to come to us , so we can assist with the small things.

We deal with disruptions immediately, since if we don't take action this now, when will we? It's essential to be available to those whom you interact with and live with, but don't be spending all of your daytime hours helping them , when you have your own work to complete. It is better to focus on the needs of your personal life, be aware of your limits and refrain from rushing around. That's why you need to tell yourself "no".

Bob Carter once said "Poor planning on your behalf does not warrant an emergency in mine". Sometimes, you may be tempted to respond to a request from a colleague, however, you must recognize the time when it is appropriate to stop what you're doing to help and be able to be able to say "no" to be able to effectively manage your work.

Is My Stuff Taking Over My Life?

A lot of people be plagued with clutter. There are a lot of magazines and papers, overflowing garages stuffed with unopened boxes closets that look like department stores and on. This is a major issue due to the inability of being organised and feeling like "the things" is taking over our personal identity. The desire to have multiple things has certain negative consequences. Children are overwhelmed by their collection and they lose the capacity to concentrate or focus. The financial burden is piled up due to unaccounted for bills and a tendency to buy too much. The couple never is able to resist the urge to let go of their belongings. The same thing happens.

Controlling the home is a crucial first step. While there are dangers out there, security in the home can guarantee peace and security. peace. The mess can be difficult and stressful however, if you can eliminate the issue of mess, all will be well.

Are Stress bad?

If you are stressed the body produces defense chemicals and increases the activity of your immune cells , which boost defense. Your brain and body receive an increase in their activity due to this. The stress-inducing burst can, as you may have guessed can ward off diseases as well as make vaccinations more effective and can even help protect you from certain kinds of cancer. A small amount of stress can improve your memory. However, excessive stress is a negative thing. It's the reason there has to be an equilibrium. A low level of stress isn't enough to increase the body's defense mechanisms and could cause you to be bored. If you're stressed too much, you'll be tired, cranky and sick.

What do I do when I feel anxiety?

Sometimes it's better to admit that you're experiencing anxiety and concentrate on what's before you. If you try to block or ignore it will only make the experience more intense. If you're in an the office, at a party or other social gathering, get in touch and pay attention to the conversation. Be aware of your words when you are given the opportunity to speak. If you're experiencing anxious, you should try to confront the issue head-on. Make sure you breathe deeply every now and then often, allowing the anxiety to fade off.

How Can I Stop Focusing at the Timer?

It's akin to a religious practice of removing yourself from the world of time. getting rid of your perception of time requires removing the ego you have created.

The first step to do this is to get beyond"the "time dimension" whenever you can. Make it a habit to be in the present moment. Try to focus on the events that occurred before or is to come as they are irrelevant to the moment right now.

Step two is to stay aware in your head. Be conscious of your thoughts, feelings and reactions to various situations. You should be at least as curious about your reactions to specific situations or individuals.

The third and last step is to engage your senses completely. Take a look around but don't take in the things you observe. Take note of the area that accommodates all things. Be aware of the sounds and to the silence. Feel anything you touch and feel its Being.

It might not make sense however, the more you disengage and detach yourself from time and the clock it is easier to relax and enjoy yourself.

Chapter 15: importance of Taking Breaks

Now, think about how many breaks you have every day, and how the length of each break will last (on an average). Are you the type of person who sets aside large chunks of time that are devoted to work and then attempt to accomplish as much as you can within the time frame, or are you the type of person who would work for a while, then take a quick break, then work longer, take a second short break, do an additional bit, take another break and so on?

Breaks are essential to getting more productive and properly manage your time. It is true that you shouldn't take too frequent breaks to the point that they reduce the time you can spend actually doing things However, it is recommended to have a number of breaks per every day.

If you're feeling emotionally and physically exhausted at the conclusion of your day, it's an obvious sign there's a problem with taking the right time off. When you feel physically and mentally exhausted at the beginning it becomes more difficult to get the work accomplished.

Regular breaks of 5-10 minutes are enough to give your body relaxation and rest to allow you to return to the flow of things. As a principle it is recommended that you establish an habit to take at least a 5-10 minute break every hour you work.

It's likely result in roughly an hour (or maybe a bit more) of your day which you could have been working. So why not invest that hour doing more work? There are many reasons to have a 10-minute break each hour of work. Here are the top reasons:

Breaks can boost productivity

Numerous studies have almost proved that people who take a brief break for an hour are likely to have higher level of productivity over those who do not. The reason is that when you are working continuously and take only one or two lunch breaks and your brain can turn dull. This means that your job is increasingly less valuable to your. Your energy is exhausted and you could be able to complete your job like a robot rather than a person.

Pause for a moment so that you can relax and then come back with a fresh perspective. This is the reason those who schedule five to 10 minutes of breaks for each hour of work are not just going to be able to accomplish more in any given day and their tasks will also be of better quality too.

Breaks can help you be more creative

The short breaks you take every hour will not only increase your productivity It also makes you more imaginative! Did we mention earlier that working for a long time can make your brain dull? If you work in this manner, you'll be much less likely to getting a fresh perspective on things. However, if you stop and let your mind refresh it will be able to take the task back with an entirely different view. Imagine a 5-10 minute break as a chance to refreshment for your brain in order to boost your levels of creativity.

Breaks are good for your Physical Health

Humans, as a species, aren't built to sit at an office for the entire day. It is essential to be active and moving around. This ensures that blood circulation is maintained and that our brain gets more oxygen. Just walking around your office for five minutes after each working hour is beneficial for your physical health.

Breaks Give You The Chance To Engage In Something Positive

If we say to take breaks We don't suggest that you sit up and stretch out and grab another drink. We're referring to the need to engage in something stimulating. A short activity, but one that stimulates your mind.

You must now to get off your chair and walk around. This is a fact. However, you must be more than just taking your new drink and checking email. Perhaps instead, you can use a short but fun app on your smartphone which stimulates your brain to be able to think or to be able to respond quickly. You could also make use of the time to think about ideas for a different project you're working on as a pastime.

Breaks Offer You A Change Of Scenery

Last but not least, your computer and desk aren't not the most inspiring surroundings do you think? Take advantage of your breaks to take a chance to escape your workplace and have a fresh environment. The new surroundings will always be better for you if you're outside instead of the dull inside office. A walk for five minutes can be a great experience for your mind as well as your body, and can help get you going for the rest of your work.

Chapter 16: Time Management The Relationship Between Productivity and Success - What's the Link?

Did you know that workplace interruptions cost companies around $588 billion because of reduced efficiency in the US every year (Brown 2015)? The essence of productivity is being productive. It's about making something happen. It's about making an effort to achieve a purpose. It's all about the ability to accomplish and being actionable. However, sometimes despite our best efforts and best intentions we don't always succeed in being efficient. We've experienced the days when we couldn't accomplish anything, regardless of the amount of effort and time we invest. Our minds can't wrap around anything or remain focussed. This is what we refer to as obstacles to productivity, and they can be a lot. We've already covered the top ones earlier in the chapter We will concentrate on those that we haven't yet discussed and examine their negative effects upon our capability to function to our fullest capacity.

Obstacles to Productivity

Resignation from Work

The research conducted by the AXA PPP healthcare revealed that 42% of employees in small businesses are blaming disinterest or absence of enthusiasm for their job as the main reasons for their lack of productivity. The more sophisticated our technology are, the less interested we are with our jobs. Despite having the best productivity-enhancing apps and time-tracking metrics, our rate of productivity is declining overall. More surprising is that nearly two-thirds of businesses do track productivity. However, is it not also logical it is the monotonier our work is, the lower our productivity? In addition to being bored, a variety of other factors affect productivity. They include:

Poor Communication

Face-to-face communications have been more fragmented than it has ever before. While calling someone and engaging in video chats take under a minute unlike the past, communication has become more unclear. They're not as precise and can send mixed messages. This could affect productivity. Communication issues cost businesses millions of dollars every year because things delay when plans haven't been properly coordinated or have a discrepancy that requires changing. Let's take the marketing industry as an example. How often has it occurred that the client does not like the concept and the designer must revise the design from scratch costing time and money? If communication has become fluid, shouldn't they also be able to get the job perfect on the first try? It's not a surprise that, the more changes we're required to make more, the lower our efficiency becomes.

The issue of miscommunication, a different form in poor communications, can be a more serious problem. Communication issues can be a problem at the same time, as well. Employees might not have the necessary information and may not want to seek clarification, which results in low quality of work as well as wasted precious time as well as energy. Insufficient communication between employees and employer could also result in an increase in productivity, and can disrupt the workplace environment and the relationships.

A poor working environment

We all work best in different work conditions. Some need a quiet environment for concentration, while others are drawn to the sound of their surroundings and therefore they work outside the walls of their workplace and into cafes or malls. They seem to be awed by chaos and are skilled at how to block out the background noise and yet being able to stay clear of distractions. Unsuitable working space, whether it's bad people, poor lighting or simply crowded spaces that make us feel uncomfortable sitting in our chairs and it hinders our performance. Therefore, we must make sure that the workplace is free from all kinds of clutter to allow us to concentrate better and achieve better results. We must create a space that won't allow distractions to take over our work. That means that we need to keep a distance between ourselves and our electronic devices, as well. The presence of a television in your living room constantly will not do much to your productivity. It will only bring it down, as it keeps distracting your attention with its vivid colors and breaking news section. In the same way, the wrong temperature could cause problems in your work. If you experience hot or cold each when someone turns on or off the AC closest your home, this could frustrate you and cause you to lose concentration.

Unorganized Workstations

Like the one above cluttering up your desk or workspace can be a major deterrent to efficiency. It is easy to break the flow of work by rummaging through the mess or getting caught in charging cables. It is essential to ensure everything is in order before beginning.

Demotivating Benefits

In the past in the past, the only thing that interested applicants for a job was whether it was compatible with their passions, or not. It was okay to be payed less, as long as they could perform what they liked doing. This led to the creation of no-pay internships and people was drawn to affiliating them with organizations that they believed in. These were the people who were ready to work hours, work more work, pay for their travel expenses and return home with a smile. But no longer.

Nowadays, people are following their passions less , and make cash more. They're willing to switch careers when an opportunity to make a difference comes along. There's a lack of integrity and loyalty to the business. The employees aren't the ones to blame but the management is. They're not offering anything appealing enough to have employees consider a second thought before making the change. They're not offering enough bonuses and the appraisals are biased , and the culture isn't great also. All of this causes low productivity in the workplace because employees are focused on getting their pay and not concerned about how well or how poorly they are doing for the business. They're not willing to go above and over and above the call of duty to make their company more successful. What employers must do is provide exciting rewards that employees cannot resist. Incentives are the right of employees since it's a clear indication that they would like to be valued and recognized for what they do. If they aren't feeling that way they aren't going to be able to perform at their highest level.

The lack of training

The lack of proper training is another reason that individuals have difficulty remaining productive. There aren't all employees who are hired by the company with the best level of knowledge. There are many things that are acquired on the job. There are times when we excel in certain capabilities, but not in allof them, that's why we're always a student. In the fast pace at which changes in the workplace the training and development department has become an integral part of almost all large companies. The weaknesses and lack of experience can be addressed to fill them with training. But, if the business does not provide this training the training, it could be a hindrance to productivity. If employees don't have the necessary knowledge or ability to do an assignment and aren't able to do their best work or be productive. They're more likely to fail or not be able to complete the task.

The Management of Time and Productivity

It is possible to get distracted by external factors like distractions, conversations with staff and other distractions like unexpected tasks, meetings, emails pop-ups and social media. All of these are tasks which you're not expected to complete and therefore the time you spend doing these things isn't ethical also. Did you know that many of these tasks are personal and take about 40% of the time we work? This was discovered by a company that makes management software known as Workfront chose to conduct a survey of more than 2,010 workers who were working eight-hour shifts every day (Renzulli 2019,). The main goal of the survey was to find out how much time workers were working the work they were compensated for and the amount of time was not being recorded every year. 40% is equivalent to three hours for each eight-hour shift, that leaves us with five hours of work that is productive. The 60%, or five hours is further broken down into these categories.

A quarter of time is spent checking emails and responding.

*12% of time is spent performing administrative tasks.

* 10 percent of the time, we take part in beneficial meetings, while eight percent of our time, we're forced to attend unwelcome meetings.

* 8percent part of that time used in interruptions, and the rest 6% is used elsewhere.

However, there is one person who, despite all the interruptions, is able to get everything done on their list. They're always submitting their projects before deadlines, showing prepared for presentations and presenting the most innovative ideas that could only be the result of extensive research and analysis. How do they manage this and why aren't us? They work the same number of time in the day to get up and work. How can they be superior to us?

The subject was of interest to a senior lecturer, Robert C. Pozen at the MIT Sloan School of Management. He conducted a survey of more than 20,000 people across six continents in order to get an understanding of why certain people could accomplish more, while others did not. Contrary to what many believe that they were not working additional or extended hours, they were simply doing their work more effectively. What exactly does that mean? Being smarter is about getting the most important work removed first, and then using the extra time to tackle other or less crucial tasks. They planned better and prioritizing their tasks more effectively. The research was released in Harvard Business Review and helped transform the thinking of many employees and managers around the world (Pozen and Downey, 2019,).

Professionals who value working smarter than working harder scored higher in the study. They were adept at making plans and setting priorities according to. They developed strategies and strategies which helped them filter through the vast amount of data and comprehend the requirements of their colleagues as well.

What is recommended for becoming productive ? There are some habits which are simple to master and modify, according to by the results of the survey. They include:

• Revision of daily action plans and rescheduling important events accordingly.

Make sure you have everything planned out at night so that you are able to get to work knowing what you need to do.

* Learn how to prioritize your tasks based on their importance and urgency.

Use calendars, to-do lists and planners to record important events as well as messages or tasks.

When you're beginning something, you should spend the initial five minutes writing down the plan and the way you'll follow each step.

* Develop a rational sequence of actions to ensure that everything is in the flow. It shouldn't be necessary to return or skipping a few steps to complete the task at hand.

• Set aside a certain period of time to look at your phone's screens as well as your computers. Make sure you don't check them every minute.

* Don't respond to every email in the order they arrive. Prioritize them according to who sent them and the need for a quick response.

Keep meetings short and focused. Everyone who attends will

have received a written notice at least a day prior to the meeting to ensure they know the topics to be discussed.

The Management of Time, the Happiness and a Boosted Productivity

Our mood can have a major influence on our productivity as well. When we're not overwhelmed or angry, it is possible to focus better and consequently perform better. This concept was further developed by the writer of the best-selling book Stumbling on Happiness, Daniel Gilbert. As per the author, Mr. Gilbert, a wandering or unfocused mind can be neither productive or happy. He says that since we're so easily multitasking, we aren't able to complete tasks on time and do not make the most of the 45 percent of our daytime. If we are constantly switching between things or think about them all at once our minds wander off in different directions. This kind of wandering produces nothing of value and increases the stress levels and makes us feel unsatisfied.

To be more content and productive, we have be able to keep the time we have at our highest level. We must be sure to avoid doing anything that allows our minds the opportunity to wander and create anxiety. According to a study that was published by The Journal of Happiness, people who are able to manage their leisure time effectively enjoy a higher level of happiness (Wang, Kao, Huan and Wu 2011,).

What can we do to make it happen? Laura Vanderkam has the answer. In her book, she writes What the most successful people do on the Job: A Quick Guide to Changing your Career, that the most successful individuals consider their time as capital. They are constantly, aware of where they spend their time. They've decided to remain wealthy , and thus they spend the majority of their time doing activities that bring them closer to their goals.

Cal Newport also seems to follow the same guidelines. The well-known author of Deep Work and the owner of the Study Hacks Blog, Cal believes that one of the reasons that individuals achieve great success so effortlessly is due to the habit of planning their entire working day. It can be difficult initially but once you've mastered the habit of planning every minute of the day you'll be amazed at how easy it is when you've got everything figured out. While you're doing it you come to the realization of any deadlines or dates that you may have missed and add them to your list of things to do list. Also, if you have only a few time slots for each project and have another task scheduled you're less likely to delay and are more likely to be determined to finish it.

Controlling Time, Attention span and Productivity

Larry Rosen, a research psychologist and educator, researched the connection between focus span and productivity of students (Stringer 2017). He wanted to understand the effects of technology on the lives of students and whether it could help them achieve tasks faster or not. When he did gather around 260 middle school or high school students as well as university students for the purpose of an investigation, he discovered that the disadvantages of technology were disguised as benefits and were the root of inattention deficits and absence of concentration in the children. In the course of the experiment, students who participated were asked to sit at home and study during 15 minutes. For the duration of 15 minutes their reactions were observed. Rosen observed that it took all students under 6 minutes to become distracted and move on to another activity or distract. The most common alerts came in form of text messages phone call, vibration on the phone or beep, or even an alert. He also said that it wasn't only these notifications, but that students themselves were able to access their devices with or without alerts. Rosen said that despite the fact that technological advances were made to enhance our learning and abilities, they were actually in the exact opposite direction. Not only did students spend a lot of time reading their messages, they also didn't perform. This means that productivity was directly dependent on distractions. The more distracted the environment, the lower the productivity. The lower the productivity and the longer time is wasted.

It was also pointed out that we can't multitask. If we thought we were able to then we were mistaken. We simply changed different tasks. The first task got more important when we switched tasks and then when we came back on it we had lost some time trying to recall the place we were in and move on from there.

Thus, the aim should be to reduce distractions and to increase our focus. If our attention span is increased we'll be less susceptible to distractions, which, in turn, will hopefully will save time. The best method to achieve this is to establish a schedule that you can engage with friends. Begin by taking breaks between and checking messages and notifications for a certain period of time. When you're done then return to what you did with total concentration. Another option is to eliminate all distractions completely. If that's not feasible then you may want to turn them off for a while and make sure they are kept a safe separation from the room.

Timing Management, distractions and Productivity

Have you ever thought that an act of distraction can cause our minds to resemble the mind of a person who has smoked marijuana? According to a British study, employees experience a drastic loss of IQ when they are distracted. This is higher than the reduction in IQ of a person who smokes marijuana.

Another study conducted in conjunction with TNS Research aimed at finding the impact of continuous interruptions via telephone calls and emails. Continuous interruptions cause one to lose time, feel exhausted and lower productivity. The study included 1,100 Britons. In the course of the survey, the following data emerged.

* Two-thirds of users check their phones for official messages during holidays or outside of office hours.

They respond quickly to emails, and are more likely to respond within an hour after receiving them.

* One in five people take time off from social gatherings in order to respond to messages or phone calls during work hours.

Nine people believed that coworkers who when they were in contact were attentive to the messages of their colleagues were disrespectful. Ten of them believed it was a snub and an indication of inefficiency and lack of tenacity.

In revealing these, we realize that them can have a direct effect on productivity, and can cause us to miss valuable time. A proper management of time, and the elimination of interruptions that occur beyond working hours must be the prioritised as the top concern. There shouldn't be any obligation to answer messages received in the evenings and individuals who do this aren't rewarded more than others or considered successful people. Businesses should put their money into instructing their employees and staff members to maximize the hours they work and put off on emails and messages that are received outside of work hours. Another reason why it is important to do this is that when people stay so focused on their tasks, their mental acuity and mental clarity decrease. They become distracted by other things and consider them to be unimportant. But anything that isn't related to work is insignificant. Thus, it is essential to strive to achieve a work-life equilibrium.

Productivity and success

It is believed to be one of the key relationships which the study is built on. Are success and productivity related? If yes, do they depend or are they independent and what are the factors that can affect the rate? In addition, what part is time management playing in the whole process? However, before we go into all of that, we need to look at the definition of success. What exactly is success? Is there a common definition? Does it refer to only achievements that are related to work? Can it be achieved? Do you have metrics to measure it? Are you able to track it continuously?

Success may refer to different things for individuals. In reality, when we hear that someone is referred to for being successful, our brain immediately envisions someone who has luxurious automobiles, big houses with private yachts, extravagant watches and even suits. If it's nothing more than the ability to make money this is rather harsh.

Webster's dictionary gives an explanation of the word "accomplishment": achievement of a goal or objective.

If we look at the definition of the word "purpose" or goal is important. But not everyone wants to make money. Others just desire fame, love, or to be recognized as who they truly are. They would like to pursue their passions as that's the only thing that matters for them. Many want to live their life helping and caring to other people. It seems like that is their aim or goal. The first thing we have to comprehend is that a reason could be anything at all and the achievement of this goal is what true success looks like. In general terms it's what helps one to appreciate life and feel happy.

Don't get us wrong. We're not fighting over the definitions of the word "wealth" and wealth, but we'd rather examine the numerous possibilities of definitions it could be used to mean. It should be a sign of success, triumph, or achievement in any form, not only the word "wealth. Since neither of the definitions we have discussed previously used the terms money, wealth, or luxury. Therefore, there's the possibility that someone without an estate can be successful without the luxury of a fortune. In addition, there is no standards for measuring the extent of success. In addition, the definition of success isn't based on any time limit neither. You may be able to feel success one day, and fail the next. Success is defined by what we are able to accomplish in just a single day. It's all about whether we are able to achieve the goals and goals that we set out for ourselves, or not. This was further supported by Andy Frisella, a famous podcaster and influencer. According to Andy his definition of success, it is the achievement of one's potential (Frisella 2017, 2017). Let's take a look at this by taking it apart. Andy says that being successful in something requires actively looking for improvement and tap the full potential. This can only be achieved if you are constantly working toward the long-term goals they have set for themselves. Continuously working is about working all day and making the most of the available time available to work. Therefore, it all comes to how timing is organized and how much can be done during that time. If we're not making progress each day and achieving the daily goals we set, then we're not pursuing being successful. In contrast when we're working only half-heartedly and are not performing at our full potential is also limiting our chances of achieving success. Thus, success is defined as the combination of productivity and effective time management since both are the most important factors in all the definitions within the subsection.

The connection we were looking for been at our fingertips constantly. We were only behind in identifying it.

There has also been a lot of discussion about the three of them being dependent with each other. Why is that, you might think? We know that time is an important resource due to the fact that Benjamin Franklin told us so. And then, Brian Tracy notched it up and said that it was inexpensive and non-perishable. Understanding that time management is the key to productivity and achievement can help us see it from a different point of view and appreciate it. We are aware that we could watch all day on TV , but not actually going to work or do any chores and yet we don't. Even during the weekend, when we are given the chance to do this and we do so, we get involved with any tasks that remain. Why? Becausewe subconsciously realize that the time we've spent watching television won't last. Therefore, we put it to use on things that are more important and leave us feeling a sense of satisfaction. This is only possible when we see time as a finite resource and take pleasure in every minute of it. Why is that? It does all the following for us.

Time Management leads to improved Health

If we are healthy both physically and mentally it is easier to perform. It is not necessary for a study to discover the reasons for this. The chances of us performing better improve. The thing that many don't realize is that stress can be fatal literally (Hartz-Selley 2014). Stress is frequently connected to an increase in heart rate and blood pressure, as well as cancer, cirrhosis of liver, and lung diseases. Stress directly affects the brain and is the cause of irregularities in blood sugar. This decreases our immunity, and makes it take longer to get better.

Management of stress and time are in sync. If time management is done well it makes you feel more at ease. If you feel more in control, you are able to work at a faster pace and remain focused. This means that there are no late-night surprises and deadlines being completed in time. When you are well, you're more confident and ready to tackle any situation.

Time Management Helps you Accomplish More

If time-sucking is one of your top pet peeves, it is crucial to be focused and remove distractions. Distractions are eliminated, which means more work can be completed by the time you finish the work day. That will help you reach your objectives. Doesn't that sound like the concept of success? If you can do it with proper control of time, the success can become an actuality. This happens because people know what they want , and therefore do not lose their tempo. You're in a better position to not get distracted and complete every task to complete your day with a clear and concise way.

If you take the control over your schedule,, you will be able to improve your ability to concentrate and remove distractions. This, in turn, makes your work more efficient (Maddox 2019, 2019).

Time Management Lowers Rework

Because of the concepts that govern time, once we start to organize our time effectively it is easier to avoid the occurrences of re-work or errors. However, that doesn't mean managing your time will make you an expert, it helps you make up those gaps and loops you are likely to overlook when you're managing your time badly. This is the case when you have a list of tasks or an action plan that you have in place with each task being assigned an established time. If you know precisely the amount of time each task will take and have all the required steps set out, there's very little room for redundancies.

Time Management Enhances Decision Making

When faced with making crucial decision at the last moment there are many who feel under pressure. This can result in anxiety and panic and crucial information could be ruminated over. If time is effectively managed there's not much to be concerned about, so you are able to relax and think about all the data you require in order to take an educated choice.

The Management of Time Boosts Reputation

Tell us what people consider you if you always last to show up, or you keep slipping up on deadlines? Your reputation will certainly suffer and your goal to become successful will only be.

Everyone hates working with a person who isn't reliable and insecure. When you're able to efficiently manage time and you show on time, keep on track and get everything done by the deadline. This is a trait that employers appreciate for their employees.

Time Management Leaves you with free Time

While time management won't miraculously boost the number of hours you can work that you work however, it will help you maximize your time. If you are spending your scheduled working hours working and then you have some time to relax at the final. This is your time to relax and that you are free to spend in any way you want. It is a time to tidy up the clutter at the station, look through your emails, make private calls, or head home to spend time with your loved ones. It's a great method to relax and feel confident that you've completed everything you scheduled in the morning.

The final reason you should seriously think about managing your time is because Belinda Weaver, in her book, describes ineffective time management as the route to hell and no one wants to be there!

Chapter 17: The Habits Of Effective Time Managers

The thing is, you will not learn how to manage your time in a matter of hours. Nobody does and not even those whom you look up to as guidance. Your most beloved idols had their own mistakes but they gained knowledge from their mistakes. They were even less fortunate than you and now look at where they are today. We're talking about individuals who are like Benjamin Franklin, Maya Angelou, Oprah Winfrey, Steve Jobs or Albert Einstein. All of them had to confront the most difficult of circumstances and take on the status quo and keep their eyes on their goals. They pursued their passions and put in the time to give it their 100% and became legends. While they were from different families, ethnicities, backgrounds or generations all shared one thing they all had in their common. They were devoted to their time. They didn't spend it on sham friendships or meaningless relationships. Instead, they dedicated their energy to creating things that happened. They made a difference in the world in a positive way. It is because of these that we have the ability to take advantage of many luxury items in our lives and technological advances.

If they could do it, you can too. It's too dramatic for me to quote but it's an actual fact. The time was not as advanced as the technology we enjoy today. Many of them did not have access to the Internet or had wealthy families that supported them. They were self-made since they had a clear idea of what they wanted, and pursued it with no shame. Of sure, there were hurdles they had to conquer but they planned everything. They knew from the beginning that what they set themselves up for wouldn't be able to be an easy task. They set out to remain efficient and were able to live up to their word!

If you're going to begin, it should start today. Be productive to ensure that you can be successful in exactly the way it found them. Find ways to organize your time better. It's going to be a long process at first however, at the very the very least, you'll get on the correct track. As you'll be creating several new habits it is best to conduct a quick assessment of where you are currently. It is important that you recognize the behaviors and habits you'll must improve and keep an eye on as well as those you must beware of or abandon.

Personality Types of Time Management

Discover which personas is a match for you, so you will be able to identify the traits and actions you must work on and improve your ability to manage the precious resource of time.

Are you a firefighter?

You are the only one who, as you see it is an emergency responder? Aren't you the one who is the first to arrive at the scene of the situation while everyone else appears to be running away from it? If you're someone who is quick to get to the scene and helps make things better, is regarded as trustworthy and does not like the idea of wasting time, then it is what makes you an emergency responder. Your approach to work might not be the best since you're always moving between the lines and causing chaos in the lives of other people however, your main aim is to maximize any time to spare. This is a trait that is admired by many and worth pursuing. You are a risk-taker, however, the majority of these are planned.

There is however one flaw with the firefighter persona. Sometimes, they're so absorbed by everything that is their immediate surroundings that they misinterpret not urgent tasks as urgent too. There are always tasks that could be put off until an additional time or assigned but because they behave as people who take action, they tend to have the habit of putting their time into every single thing, even if they aren't in need of it.

Are you a Multitasker?

Are you able to handle a call while be able to sign important documents, while simultaneously reading them? If yes your time management style is what we refer to as multitaskers. At first, it may seem like a great ability to possess but it's not in the long term. Why? because multitasking has more to do with myth than fact. We think that we're multitasking, but really we're shifting between two tasks very fast. This can lead to repetition, which isn't an excellent trait to have. If you've thought that by multitasking you'll be able to complete the majority off your list completed, you should think twice. There are chances that you made mistakes in the process that require reworking. If that's the case then what's the purpose to save time when you'll be doing the corrections later?

Are You an over-committer?

Is there someone in your life who is a"yes" to everything and anyone every single day? If yes, then you're a person we refer to the term "over-committer. A person who is an over-committer is troubled by limits. They tend to be people-pleasers and are always performing other's tasks to the exclusion of their own. All you need to request their help or invite them to a party and they'll be there for you.

They are in a position of being unable to meet their obligations that is not good. They end up suffering from bad press and, when it is time to complete their work they're exhausted. In the end, there's only so much you can complete during the course of a day.

Are You Underestimating Yourself?

You are someone who often encounters the following phrases?

"I only need to take a few minutes."

"I will finish this in ten minutesor less, not much more."

"You will be able to have the report on your desk in a matter of minutes."

A person who is under-estimated is not able to manage time effectively. They don't meet their deadlines and often seek extensions. They say it's only going to take some minutes, but they'll not arrive until an hour later , and cause inconvenience to others as well.

Conclusion

Time is always limited in its resources. If you don't make the most of your time can cause you to dread it in the future. The book we've tackled several of the prevalent and persistent issues people face when it comes to time management. People complain that they don't have enough time or the energy to accomplish the tasks they would like to do. However, here's the truth: you will need to evolve. The clock never stops and is a constant. What you do to maximize your time is a skill that we intended to help you master. The only way to succeed in your daily life is if you take time as seriously as it should be , and make use of it effectively. In the ideal scenario, invest it doing important things to ensure that when you look back you're not disappointed by the things you've abandoned later in your life.

I hope that the suggestions shared in this book can help you make time work in an efficient and effective manner. Before we say goodbyes, what about doing the quick review of the topics that were discussed within the publication to freshen your mind? Let's look at how many do you remember.

In the very first chapter, we talked about what management is, and then took the time to go through the history of the point where we began tracking time. We then moved to talk about the innumerable advantages of time management and later, we determined if you are a time-waster or not.

In the following chapter, we discussed the most frequent and avoidable time-wasters. We also found out if we are able to avoid tempting situations or not.

www.ingramcontent.com/pod-product-compliance
Lightning Source LLC
Chambersburg PA
CBHW071124130526
44590CB00056B/1915